Ian Buxton

101 World Whiskies to Try Before You Die

Ian Buxton

101 World Whiskies to Try Before You Die

First published in 2012
by HACHETTE SCOTLAND, an imprint of HACHETTE UK

1

Cataloguing in Publication Data is available from the British Library
978 0 7553 6319 3

Designed by Lynn Murdie
Cover design by Chris Hannah
Printed and bound in Thailand by Imago

HEADLINE PUBLISHING GROUP
An Hachette UK Company
338 Euston Road
London NW1 3BH

www.headline.co.uk
www.hachette.co.uk

Contents

Introduction   7

101 whiskies   14

How to taste whisky and use this book   218

Further resources   219

Where to buy   221

Acknowledgements   223

Cartoon postcard, ca. 1906. Plus ça change.

Introduction

What? *Another* 101 Whiskies? Are you serious?

Well, yes, actually – for two reasons.

Firstly, people were kind enough to ask for another dip into the great lucky bag of whisky and secondly, and more significantly, much has changed in the world of whisky, even since the last book was published (August 2010). Changed for the better, you'll be glad to hear.

But perhaps you didn't buy the first book[1].

> This is a whisky list with a difference. Accessible whisky for real people.
>
> It is not an awards list.
>
> It is not a list of the 101 'best' whiskies in the world. It is simply, as it says in the title, a guide to 101 whiskies that enthusiasts really should seek out and try – love them or hate them – to complete their whisky education. What's more, it's practical and realistic.

Well, that was the idea. Since you've asked for more, I presume it worked.

Because so much is happening in the world of whisky, I've been able, with a clear conscience, to make an entirely new selection of 101 whiskies. That doesn't mean that I no longer endorse my previous choices (quite the opposite, in fact) but, with so much that is exciting, it's possible to present a completely up-to-the-minute collection. What is more, unlike the previous recommendations, I've tried to avoid multiple expressions from the same brand. Some distilleries crop up again and again, however, especially in the USA where it is fairly common practice for different, sometimes competing, brands to emerge from the same distillery. Don't worry, they taste different.

There has been a trend in recent years (which is accelerating alarmingly) towards ever more expensive whiskies. Where, not so long ago, the idea of a whisky costing £1,000 a bottle would have been ludicrous, it's now, if not commonplace, a frequent occurrence.

The £1,000 bottle has become the £10,000 bottle. Yes, really. You may think it absurd that for the price of a single bottle of whisky you could buy a brand spanking new Fiat 500, drive it to a decent off-licence, put some very fine drams in the boot and still have change from £10,000 – and I would agree with you – but the £10,000 bottle is out there.

[1] Don't worry, it's still available if you'd care to snap up a copy – and you should!

And are you really going to nip out and buy one?

Didn't think so.

But it doesn't stop there. There are whiskies offered at £100,000 a bottle now and the idea of buying whisky as an 'investment' is being seriously proposed. You may think that sounds horribly reminiscent of the fable of the Emperor's New Clothes, and I'd agree – this is something I'll address later.

A Charmed Life

Meanwhile, back to the book. Whisky writers lead a charmed and privileged life. We get to taste many, if not all, of these fabulous and exotic releases. Delightful PR people transport us to private rooms in fashionable and expensive restaurants where their distillery clients lead us through their limited releases, special editions and rare or exclusive drams. Then, as often as not, we eat a carefully prepared meal and, late in the evening, having enjoyed ourselves mightily at their expense, we depart with a gift – as if turning up on time and paying attention were some kind of hardship. Long may all that continue … But it's hardly the world in which most people live. In the era of the World Wide Web and the instant gratification that you can get from it, there seems to me little point in writing about whiskies that sell out in days, or which the overwhelming majority of the readership can't find, let alone afford[2].

So I set myself some rules when I started writing the first book and I've carried them over into this volume. Essentially, every whisky listed here must be: a) generally available: although you might have to look a little bit, almost every one of these whiskies can be bought from a decent whisky specialist or through an online retailer[3]; and b) affordable (read on to see what that means).

And it goes without saying that there must be an excellent reason for their inclusion. Mostly it's because they are very, very good examples of their kind, but sometimes they deserve your attention for other reasons – they might be made by small distillers swimming against a tide of corporate ubiquity, or it could just be because a whisky is so unusual you just have to try it. Perhaps a certain whisky will remind you of something familiar that you already knew about but had, sort of, forgotten? Hopefully, most entries will point you towards something new, unexpected and surprising.

[2] Note to PR industry: don't stop inviting me, though. I will mention your clients elsewhere. Honest.

[3] One or two aren't yet; that's not to challenge your ingenuity, more to encourage the relevant distiller to supply a wider market.

A New World of Whisky

This time, though, I've deliberately spread my net further and wider. This is what I meant at the beginning when I wrote that much has changed. In the last two or three years, the availability of whisky from around the world has grown dramatically. A few years ago a number of small distillers from countries far and wide set out, generally quite independently but also coincidentally, to prove that they could distil whisky every bit as well as the traditional whisky nations of Scotland, Ireland and the USA.

After all, a huge amount of whisky is drunk in France where great Cognacs and Armagnacs suggest they know one end of a still from the other – so why not make whisky? And the Swiss distil superb fruit schnapps and the Germans are no slouches either, and so we go on. There is more domestic 'whisky' made and drunk in India than there is Scotch whisky drunk in the entire world. Most of it we would consider to be rum (it's made from molasses) but sooner or later it was bound to occur to someone that they could make single malt whisky in India to sell back to Scotland.

And so they have. At first many of these 'new world' whiskies were treated with a sort of patronising indulgence by the establishment – uncomfortably reminiscent of the early attitudes to the first Japanese whiskies. But some of the New Wave have proved quite extraordinarily good and have built justifiably high reputations in a surprisingly short period of time. So let's welcome them, especially if it makes some of the old guard sharpen up.

The frustrating thing about whisky is that you have to wait quite a while until it's ready. So, although whisky aficionados knew that a whole lot of 'new' whisky was about to become available, it wasn't until very recently that you could find much of it. And because many of these new operations are quite small, their products will never be found on supermarket shelves – which, in my book, makes them all the more interesting. You'll just have to try a little bit harder to track them down. I've listed a few of the best suppliers internationally at the end of the book.

So, while in the previous book 70 of the 101 whiskies were from Scotland alone, this time I've cut Scotland back to less than one third of the list and made space for whisky from Australia, Austria and so on. It means more delicious bourbons and very special rye whiskies from the USA; obscure but delightful drams from Switzerland, Germany and Sweden; and even a (potentially) exciting expression from England!

You'll find the book is organised in alphabetical order by country, with the whiskies (where there are more than one from a particular country), arranged in the same fashion.

Fundamentally, though, this book is about whiskies to drink, not collect. For that reason, it excludes one-off bottlings, because there's simply not enough to go around and they're all gone before any book can reach the shops anyway. But, in deference to the production constraints that apply to many of the new boutique 'craft' distillers, I have included single cask releases. In some cases these whiskies sell out very quickly. Highly collectable releases can go even faster – believe it or not, all bottles of Highland Park's Earl Haakon were reputedly sold in 44 minutes. You can read about these on the many excellent blogs that have sprung up in recent years.

But I've totally ignored whiskies that appear to be designed primarily for collectors: a market which seems to me to be in great danger of being swamped with over-priced offerings. I find the idea of a whisky specifically designed for collecting rather depressing and I do wonder what the people who actually made it think about their life's work ending up on a shelf, rather than in a glass being enjoyed with friends.

Anyway, if I hadn't been selective we would have ended up with 1,001 whiskies – and who wants a book about that?

I've continued to take a very hard-headed look at retail prices. I've been picky once a whisky rises above £100 in a typical British whisky shop; very critical, indeed, if it costs £500 or more; and flatly ignored it once the price breaks the £1,000 barrier, let alone £10,000 or £100,000. (Actually, that's not strictly true – the bonus 102nd whisky is one you can't find, won't be offered and almost certainly can't afford anyway. But it's fun to read about while pretending you've won the Lottery.)

Again, the emphasis is on great value. Here's the key to the 1 to 5 scale:
☐ Under £25 ◻ £25–39 ▨ £40–69 ▣ £70–150 ■ Over £150

The price ranges are based on the typical UK retail price and were correct as we went to press. Whisky can be a serious bargain! And so much the better, since, let's get real, this book is for whisky drinkers, not Russian plutocrats. And that brings me to the topic of 'investing' in whisky.

Extraordinary Popular Delusions and the Madness of Crowds

As I write this (March 2012), there has been a flurry of breathless press reports in a number of highly respected national newspapers, to the effect that the right whisky can make a great investment. This followed some energetic PR work by a particular distiller keen to promote a particular brand and by one particular off-licence chain (as they have every right to do). But it might seem that they have a vested interest in promoting whisky as an investment – I leave that up to you to decide.

Let's begin by defining some terms. I understand why people *collect* whisky and, though I personally find that rather sterile an activity, I can see the appeal. Collecting holds out the tantalising possibility of eventual consumption, without which potential any bottle becomes devoid of meaning or significance. Collecting whisky may seem a little odd to those not bitten by the bug but it's essentially harmless and proceeds from a love of the product. However, in recent years, the value of a few collectable bottles (not all) has risen sharply, leading some collectors to suggest that they are 'investing' in whisky – which is rather different from buying whisky purely as an investment.

I also happen to believe that writers and journalists have a duty of care to their readers. If I write, 'Try the Tannochbrae 10-year-old, it's delicious', then that's simply my opinion and the worst that can happen is that you buy a bottle and you don't particularly like it. But if I start recommending Tannochbrae 10-year-old as 'an investment' we've moved to a new, dangerous and rather depressing place. 'Investment' is a loaded word and should, in my view, be used carefully and sparingly. That hasn't been happening lately.

We can argue about the figures, but common sense suggests that a return of over 100% in just two or three years cannot be sustained in anything but a feverish bubble. When you appreciate that those figures are being most enthusiastically trumpeted by distillers with a brand to promote, retailers with stock to move or auction houses keen to drum up business, you might just want to look twice before committing your pension pot. Certainly, you should ask what motive might be behind any recommendation.

Buxton's First Law of Investment states that by the time an alternative investment idea appears in the weekend lifestyle supplements then the smart money has been made by those with an inside track and they're getting ready to move on. Guess who delivers their profits for them?

But there's a more fundamental philosophical point that the money men, with their hard, cold souls (and, sadly, a few whisky people as well) don't seem to get. Once you buy *just for investment*, as some pundits are now suggesting, then the bottle might as well contain cold tea – since, by definition, it's never going to be opened. Today whisky, tomorrow pork belly futures.

Whisky is a *drink*. But it is more than that. This book holds that – at its best – whisky is a metaphor for the spirit and soul of the people and place where it is produced. The distillers of Scotland express part of the austere, Calvinist personality of their land; in Kentucky (just as in 1786 for Rabbie Burns) 'freedom and whisky gang the gither'; and for the brave new distillers in Brittany, France, it encapsulates their Breton identity and culture, even their language. English whisky – well, perhaps there they distil a bit of the famous English dry sense of humour.

If you love whisky, set it free. Mark my words: this 'investment' bubble will end badly and some people – and whiskies – are going to get hurt.

No scores

Because I don't believe in the simplistic and reductionist notion of the 'world's best whisky', which, all too often, is only one person's opinion anyway, this book is in alphabetical order. And, even more unusually, nothing has a 'score'. Again, I simply don't accept that you should follow one person's individual preferences and more or less idiosyncratic scoring system (and that's all that most tasting books are). There are several reasons why 100-point scoring systems don't work, not least the palpably absurd idea that any one individual can consistently and reliably differentiate between a whisky scoring 92.5 and one scoring 93.

I suggested previously that it was better to take some advice from Aeneas MacDonald, the original sage of whisky, who in 1930 suggested that the discerning drinker should learn to judge whisky with 'his mother-wit, his nose and his palate to guide him'. Sound words that still ring true.

That's all folks! Enjoy the list, even if you disagree with some of it. But, most of all, enjoy the whisky.

As the poet would have it, 'Tak aff your dram!'

Ian Buxton.
March 2012.

ADNAMS.
SOUTHWOLD
COPPER
HOUSE
DISTILLERY

1

Bakery Hill
Cask Strength – Peated Malt

Producer	Bakery Hill
Distillery	Bakery Hill, Balwyn North, Victoria, Australia
Visitor Centre	No
Availability	Limited specialists and distillery
Price	▢▢▢▢

Bakery Hill

Cask Strength – Peated Malt

Right now if you could pick just one hot spot for the development of world whisky, it would be Tasmania. So, just to be perverse, Bakery Hill is located north-east of Melbourne in Victoria where they claim to operate 'Australia's premium malt whisky distillery'.

Given that there are, at today's count, at least eight others in production, that's not quite as absurd an assertion as it may appear – though I daresay that Bill Lark (widely considered the founding father of modern Australian whisky) might have something to say.

And we might, in passing, note that whisky was being distilled (by Dewar's of all people) in Australia as early as 1929, although their Corio distillery near Geelong closed in 1980. Bakery Hill started operations in 2000 and the distillery was enlarged in 2008, allowing larger volumes to be produced and small amounts to be shipped to international markets.

Interestingly, all the output is bottled as single cask releases, mainly (but not always) at cask strength[4], so chances are that if you go back for a second bottle it will be different from the one you just finished. Inevitably, given this approach, the small-scale production and the distance it has to travel to European markets, it's not cheap – expect to pay the equivalent of around £90 for a full bottle of the 46% abv versions and more for the cask strength.

What's exciting about this is just how it demonstrates the vibrancy, diversity and willingness to experiment that marks out many of the 'world' distillers; in marked contrast to the rather more staid and proscriptive Scotch whisky industry. As we are about to see, they need to watch out.

I am waiting for a sample of the Bakery Hill Peated Malt as we go to press (sorry). This is what they say:

Nose　　A rich, subdued peat aroma combined with a natural leathery earthiness, with overtones of kumquat and fruit mince tart. Sweet but not sickly.

Taste　　The palate reveals a tobacco-leaf earthiness with layer upon layer of complex smoky peat that lingers on the lips and palate demanding just one more sip.

Finish　　Astonishingly long and complex, an exotic mix of experiences.

[4] Normally whisky is sold at 40%, 43% or sometimes 46% abv (alcohol by volume) but it doesn't start out like that. It goes into the barrel at around 65% abv. Evaporation and aging generally mean that it loses strength over time and then it is usually diluted with water prior to bottling. If not, it's 'cask strength'.

Verdict

2

Producer
Distillery
Visitor Centre

Availability
Price

Lark Distillery Cask Strength
Lark Distillery
Lark, Hobart, Tasmania
Yes – escorted one- and two-day tours
Limited specialists and distillery
☐☐☐☐

www.larkdistillery.co.au

Lark Distillery
Cask Strength

Bill Lark, of the eponymous distillery, is a cheerful fellow. As well he might be. When not engaged at his own distillery, he helps fellow Tasmanians establish theirs, and also consults on possible start-ups in New Zealand and – shock, horror – Scotland.

He even helped found the Tasmanian Whisky Producers Association. With 10 members (8 distilleries and 2 independent bottling companies), it's the best possible demonstration of the vibrant craft-distilling scene that has taken root on Tasmania since he first set up in 1992. So he can justly look back with pride on his vision of a local whisky-distilling industry that can hold its head up in world company, and not for nothing is he acknowledged as the father of contemporary distilling in Australia. Today his daughter Kristy looks after the day-to-day production while Bill travels the world as a most enthusiastic and engaging ambassador.

The original site, on Hobart's waterfront, remains a shop front, with café, retail outlet and whisky bar, while the 'new' distillery has grown significantly. Their property now includes their own peat bog and cooperage.

The good news, therefore, is that supplies are reaching international markets and we can see what all the fuss is about. To be entirely honest, on first tasting this I was blown away. Lark distils from Tasmanian (Franklin) barley, which is locally malted and lightly peated. It's then double distilled in locally crafted pot stills and the heart of the run is transferred to 100 litre oak casks, where it matures for up to 8 years. That's quite a lengthy period considering the wood to liquid ratio and makes for a remarkably mature spirit.

Well done to them for their patience. Some early releases of (other) Australian whisky were, frankly, immature and if you had tried one you would look rather suspiciously on other offerings from Down Under. Fear no more! Find the Lark name on a bottle and you may be assured of its quality, even though they will vary, since everything is being released as single casks.

The bottle I tried was Cask LD100 and was 58% abv. Yum!

Nose   Sweet and malty; some smoke; floral and perfumed. Burnt toffee.

Taste   Evidently not Scotch, yet elegant, spicy, dry and peppery.

Finish   Somewhat terse. Like this tasting note.

Verdict ....

....

3

Producer
Distillery

Visitor Centre
Availability
Price

Sullivan's Cove Double Cask
Tasmania Distillery
Tasmania, Cambridge, Hobart,
Tasmania
No
Limited specialists and distillery
■■■

Sullivan's Cove

Double Cask

This was the very first Australian whisky I ever tried and it was, without a shadow of a doubt, very nasty. It was not a product that was going to trouble anyone. But that was a few years ago now and things have moved on.

New owners took control, the distillery was relocated to the present site and the initial run of whisky was quietly swept under the carpet. What they sell today, under the Sullivan's Cove name, was distilled as things had begun to improve and, though they don't declare its age, the taste suggests that the spirit has been enhanced by proper maturation.

They are also holding back stocks from 2003 onwards, with the aim of giving them a full 12 years in cask. I expect those to be really something, especially if plans for a new distillery and warehouse come to fruition.

Right now, Sullivan's Cove can be found in quite a few international markets, although, if you live in Australia, you can also buy and hold your own cask. If the distillery keeps progressing and winning awards, this may prove a shrewd buy for the enthusiast.

Most widely seen is the Double Cask, which is bottled at 40% abv (shame, really, I think a few extra per cent would really help) and represents a vatting of whisky that has been matured respectively in ex-bourbon barrels (American oak) and Port pipes (French oak). They're aiming, they say, for '*a perfect balance between sweet malt and oak that ends with a hint of dark chocolate and rainforest botanic*'. Sounds a bit like a shampoo commercial actually: an alarming thought.

There being a shortage of rainforests (but not rain) in Scotland, I'm not quite sure what that leads me to expect, but this is evidently well made and, thankfully, they've avoided the fashion for peating, so we get closer to the inherent spirit character.

In a wry glace at Tasmania's darker past, they style their whisky: 'Distilled with Conviction'. It's certainly no crime to drink it.

Nose	An initially aggressive alcohol hit (even at 40% abv) gives way to a strange aroma of mushroom cellars. Not unpleasant, but slightly odd. Maybe it's the rainforest.
Taste	Surprisingly sweet as the Port wood unwinds; then chocolate, malt and spices.
Finish	Fairly short.

Verdict ....

....

4

	Reisetbauer 7 Years Old
Producer	Reisetbauer
Distillery	Reisetbauer, Kirchdorfergut, Austria
Visitor Centre	Yes – by arrangement, phone in advance
Availability	Limited specialists
Price	▢▢▢

Reisetbauer

7 Years Old

With its long-standing tradition of small-scale fruit distilling, Austria has embraced whisky with enthusiasm and you can track down at least five craft distillers (probably more by the time you read this). I had to pick just one here, though, and, with its whisky on sale in Scotland, Reisetbauer got the nod.

Owner Hans Reisetbauer vies with the rival Waldviertler Roggenhof distillery for the title of Austria's first whisky distiller, though you might imagine being Austria's best whisky distiller was rather more important (not that I would presume to adjudicate on that thorny issue). However, Reisetbauer collected the 2011 Falstaff Spirits Trophy and was named Austria's *best* distiller, so presumably he feels vindicated by that. Certainly Reisetbauer has a well-established reputation as an excellent distiller of fruit schnapps. He claims that they are not trying to ape the style of Scotch but produce a distinctly Austrian take on whisky. It seems to be working.

Reisetbauer started distilling malt in 1995, but the first bottles weren't released until 2002. This 7-year-old has been blended from a mixture of Chardonnay and trockenbeerenauslese casks, and is actually exported quite widely. You may be able to find a 10- and 12-year-old release, as well.

We all know about Chardonnay, wife to a well-known Premier League footballer, but a word about trockenbeerenauslese. This describes a style of sweet dessert wine where the grapes have been picked by hand, one at a time, after they have been affected by 'noble rot' (*Botrytis cinerea*). Think of a particularly intense Sauternes and you start to get the idea. Before you grab a bottle, be aware that most trockenbeerenauslese wines are very expensive. For once it may actually be cheaper to stick to whisky.

Reisetbauer is a determinedly Austrian whisky: the barley comes from the owner's own four hectares of farmland; it is malted locally; and then warehoused at the distillery using exclusively casks from Austrian vineyards. Another fresh take on whisky to delight and surprise us.

Nose   Pronounced wine notes; cereal and fruit cake.

Taste   Forget Scotland… chocolate, red berries, honey and pine nuts.

Finish   Drying and faintly herbal.

Verdict

5

Producer	The Belgian Owl Single Malt
Distillery	PUR.E Distillerie company
	The Owl, Grâce-Hollogne,
	Belgium
Visitor Centre	No
Availability	Limited specialists
Price	▣▣▣

www.belgianwhisky.com

The Belgian Owl
Single Malt

Until I was able to find a bottle of the Belgian Owl 3-year-old single malt, all I had tried of this distillery's output was a small sample of new make – and, to be entirely honest, I wasn't that taken with it. So this just goes to show what 3 years' maturation in a decent cask can do.

But first a word on the distillery itself, which is located near Liège. It is, I think, unique in being based around an antique mobile still that is approximately 100 years old. A mobile still, you ask? Indeed: there is, to this day, a tradition on the Continent of travelling distillers who take their equipment on a trailer to small farms to distil fruit spirits and eau de vie. Much Armagnac is produced in this way. To my very great regret such a tradition never took root in Scotland. It's a mouth-watering thought that potentially every small farmer in Scotland could look out at a field of their own barley (or, indeed, their own orchards or raspberry cages) and contemplate drinking it in due course. Sadly, it'll never happen: the health and safety apparatchiks will see to that.

Today, however, this particular transient alembic has found a permanent home in what is Belgium's first whisky producer (there is at least one other, though their whisky, Het Anker, is not yet commercially available).

Belgian Owl was created by distiller Etienne Bouillon in October 2004 but the first releases never came on to the open market. Now, however, the distillery produces around 24,000 half-litre bottles annually, split across several expressions and limited editions. Everything is matured in first-fill ex-bourbon casks and the whisky is neither coloured nor chill filtered. Currently there are no peated expressions, though one is planned soon.

Etienne Bouillon is one of the increasingly diverse group of enthusiasts who have challenged the established wisdom that great whisky can only be made in the 'classic' whisky nations and who have followed their enthusiasm to make a dream come true. What's more, this dream has wheels.

Nose   Take a moment; this is quite delicate but complex. Fruity and floral.

Taste   Again, takes a few seconds for the light but complex fruit and honey to assert itself.

Finish   Clean and complex.

Verdict ....

....

6

**Canadian Club
Classic 12 Year Old**

Producer	Beam Inc.
Distillery	Hiram Walker, Windsor, Ontario, Canada
Visitor Centre	Yes – Hiram Walker's original home near the Distillery
Availability	Specialists
Price	▢▢

www.canadianclubwhisky.com

Canadian Club
Classic 12 Year Old

This is the global giant of Canadian whisky, sold in 150 countries around the world. It started life as the brainchild of an American entrepreneur, Hiram Walker, who in the 1870s was looking to create a whisky 'lighter than Scotch and smoother than bourbon' from his Walkerville distillery.

That became known as Club Whisky and, by the early 1880s, Canadian Club. Sales in the US were so great that the American distilling industry lobbied energetically against its import but that seems to have done little more than encourage their countrymen to drink it with even greater relish and in greater quantities. It's fair to say that the Hiram Walker Company lobbied back equally energetically, decrying the publicity directed against them in a splendidly named booklet *A Plot Against the People*[5] which was distributed in enormous quantities (it's now quite collectable).

It enjoyed a colourful association during Prohibition with bootlegger Captain William Frederick McCoy, who was not, as it turns out, the origin of the phrase 'the real McCoy', and notorious Chicago gangster Al Capone. Some claim it to be the original whisky in a Manhattan cocktail, thanks to Sir Winston Churchill's mum and a creative barman at the Manhattan Club. Or perhaps not, as Lady Churchill is also said to have been pregnant and in France at the time.

After the usual twists and turns of corporate life, it has ended up with ownership back in the USA with Beam Inc. This may or may not be a good thing for Beam: as a global brand Canadian Club delivers significant sales volume but that makes this recently independent company an attractive acquisition target for their giant competitors who have nothing Canadian in their portfolio and look on it with greedy eyes.

I suggest you lift your eyes beyond the standard version and splash out on the premium styles. The Classic 12 Year Old benefits from the extra aging. At less than £30 in the UK, it's almost a gift to the people.

[5] It has the marvellously baroque sub-title: *A History of the Audacious Attempt By Certain Kentucky 'Straight Whisky' Interests to Pervert the Pure Food Law.*

Nose   Soft and approachable. Vanilla and some citrus hints.

Taste   Some rye spice but tempered by wood notes.

Finish   Spicy notes come through.

Verdict ....

....

7

Producer
Distillery

Visitor Centre
Availability
Price

Gibson's Finest 12 Year Old
William Grant & Sons Distillers Ltd
Hiram Walker, Windsor, Ontario,
Canada
No
Limited specialists
□□

www.gibsonsfinest.ca

Gibson's Finest

12 Year Old

I loved this. It was a real surprise and a delight. But the story is rather confusing. First of all, we have one of the largely unsung parts of the William Grant empire. Then there's the tangled history and production story of Gibson's Finest, a popular Canadian whisky that started life in the USA but eventually migrated north of the border, where it moved from owner to owner and distillery to distillery in search of a permanent home.

I don't think people realise just how large and important William Grant & Sons really are. Best known for their Glenfiddich and The Balvenie single malts, they also own Tullamore Dew and the Hudson whiskey brands (Tuthilltown Spirits make these but Grants own the brands); have a very large blended whisky portfolio, and are behind Hendrick's gin and Sailor Jerry spiced rum. And their Canadian whisky doesn't get much of a press either.

So, although this is mainly available in Canada, with some supplied to the USA, I thought you should know about it. Without getting into the long and complicated history, the brand was acquired from Diageo by Grants in 2002. For some considerable time it had been produced at Schenley's Distillery in Valleyfield, Quebec, but in 2008–9 most of the blending and bottling moved to the Hiram Walker distillery in Windsor, Ontario.

It's not an expensive whisky, at least not on its home ground where it enjoys a decent market share, but don't let that put you off. In fact, some local commentators remark that it appears to have improved recently; though that's not something I'm in a position to confirm or deny.

I found it quite an agreeable and easy-to-drink whisky, adaptable in cocktails and, while it didn't blow my socks off, it certainly didn't offend. Some years ago, Dave Broom likened it (in *Whisky Magazine*) to k.d. lang[6].

So, if you're looking for a whisky that can hold a tune, this is the one for you – or is that why Canadian whisky is still something of a minority taste?

[6] Wow! We're only at number 7 and already I've managed an entirely spurious music reference. I'll make a whisky journalist yet.

Nose Spicy and herbal, with oak notes and some buttery fruit.

Taste The rye spices lead, followed by oak and vanilla. Lovely balance.

Finish Deliciously teasing spices round this off.

Verdict

8

Producer
Distillery

Visitor Centre
Availability
Price

Glen Breton Ice 10 Year Old
Glenora Distillery
Glenora, Glenville, Cape Breton,
Nova Scotia, Canada
Yes
Limited specialists and distillery
◻◻◻

www.glenoradistillery.com

Glen Breton

Ice 10 Year Old

It's been suggested by some – well, the Scotch Whisky Association to be precise – that you might confuse this with Scotch whisky. So let's be clear. This is Canadian.

As Canadian as maple syrup, Mounties and, er, other Canadian things[7]. Proudly Canadian, not Scotch. Anyway, when did you last see a Scottish distiller maturing their whisky in ice wine casks, for goodness' sake?

Never – because back in 2006 this was a world first and, given the Scotch whisky industry's aversion to anything that might diverge from 'traditional practice', you're never going to see it. But, if you can age your whisky in old Sauternes casks (and Glenmorangie and Bruichladdich, among others, do) then why not ice wine casks? At the risk of offending wine purists, and simplifying greatly, ice wine is simply a more intense dessert wine and, surprisingly, Canada makes some of the world's best around Niagara.

'Intense' is the word, though, especially as this comes at a mighty 57.2% abv. And a little goes a long way, which is perhaps why it comes in small 250ml bottles. So enjoy it in moderation. Perhaps, more candidly, you won't actually be tempted to glug it down – after dinner it could work.

I can't say it's my favourite whisky: it's just *too much*. But I love the innovation and the exploration; I love the way they acknowledge their heritage (it is Nova Scotia after all); and I love the fact they wouldn't be cowed by legal action after legal action (read about this in the first *101 Whiskies*). So buy at least one bottle. You could always give it away.

[7] Like that Celine Dion. She's Canadian. See what I did there? Another entirely irrelevant music link.

Nose   Loads of sweet tropical fruits; slightly cloying, then musty.

Taste   At the risk of being unimaginative … sweet. Maybe some dark chocolate, with hints of chilli, like those expensive chocolates you get at smart dinner parties and try to swallow with a straight face. Quickly.

Finish   I don't seem to have written anything down, so not very remarkable in any direction it would seem. Sorry.

Verdict ....

....

9

Producer
Distillery
Visitor Centre
Availability
Price

Revel Stoke Spiced Whisky
Phillips Distilling Company
A blend with some stuff in it
No
Limited specialists, if you're very lucky

www.revelstokewhisky.com

Revel Stoke

Spiced Whisky

Purists can throw their hands up in horror now and stop reading.

This is from Canada, which doesn't enjoy the greatest of reputations for its whiskies, and – the ultimately unforgivable sin – it is flavoured with spices. Lots and lots of them.

As far as Scotland is concerned, this is heresy. The idea of adding anything to flavour Scotch whisky is simply abhorrent. It just isn't entertained since, according to the guardians of the sacred flame, it is 'not traditional'; would debase the image of Scotch and do immeasurable harm to sales. Well, I think they're wrong about the first point and, as for the last two, why not let the market decide? If people don't like flavoured whiskies they'll fail and there's an end to it. Bourbon and Irish whiskey are already getting in on the act, which you might think would give the Scots pause for thought.

But there's no such bar to hold back our Canadian friends, so we can try interesting products such as Revel Stoke. Or you would if you could get it: it isn't available in the UK yet. But I have boldly put my palate at your service.

Phillips Distilling first launched this product in 2000 but it flopped. Ten years later, with emails from fans who wanted it back, and spotting the trend for American flavoured whiskies, they tried again and saw an enthusiastic reception, rather proving my point.

For the technical among us, it's distilled three times from a blend of corn, rye and barley malt. After three years of resting in charred, white oak barrels (the Canadian minimum is two), it's considered ready for the marriage with four-fold Madagascar bourbon vanilla with dashes of ginger, ground bark of cinnamon, coriander and cardamom.

In 1725, 'Fine Usquebaugh' was made using mace, cloves, cinnamon, coriander and saffron. The Victorians enjoyed 'Old Man's Milk' and, as late as the 1930s, we were drinking Highland Bitters, Het Pint and Caledonian Liquor – in all of which Scotch whisky is combined with various spices. The world didn't come to an end. Whisky seems to have survived.

Meanwhile, I suppose this is what Bailey's drinkers could try when they grow up.

Nose   Toffee and masses – *masses* – of vanilla.

Taste   Subtle it ain't. Pour over ice cream and bananas!

Finish   Rather sickly. But why not, if you like it?

Verdict ....

....

10

Producer
Distillery
Visitor Centre
Availability
Price

Hammer Head 1989 Vintage
Stock Spirits Group
Prádlo, Plzeň (Pilsen), Czech Republic
No – but visits possible if pre-arranged
UK specialists and duty free
▢▢

www.stock.cz

Hammer Head

1989 Vintage

Some pretty unusual whiskies pass over my desk and down my throat. Solely in the interest of research, naturally. They include whiskies from all around the world, but this is probably the strangest, with an unusual story to match.

This is Hammer Head, a single malt from the Czech Republic that you will see is a 1989 Vintage (it was all bottled in 2010). Don't worry if you've never heard of it; neither had I. In fact, until this arrived, I didn't even know they made whisky in the Czech Republic; although, a little research turned up the wonderfully named Gold Cock. Decided to give that one a miss.

Hammer Head turns out to be a curious, Soviet-era throwback. Just before the Berlin Wall came down, the bosses in what was then Czechoslovakia decided that whatever the capitalists could do they could do better, and set the distillers at Prádlo, in the Plzeň region, the task of making a single malt.

Plzeň is, of course, home to some of the most famous beers in the world (in 1984, I was thrown out of a brewery there with the late Michael Jackson[8]), so it's a reasonable assumption that they knew what to do with malted barley, water and yeast. They had some pot stills so whisky was duly made using Czech barley and filled into Czech oak wood casks. The wood influences around 60% of final flavour, so this is important.

But, as we all know, life changed totally with the fall of the Berlin Wall. Personnel and ownership changed at the Prádlo distillery and the single malt whisky was forgotten. The barrels just lay there; no one seems to have given them a second glance.

Now the casks have been rediscovered and are here for us to try. But this is probably a once-in-a-lifetime opportunity to taste this, or to confuse the whisky lover in your life, so you have to fly to get it – it's easiest to find in the World of Whiskies airport shops.

It's a dreadful name but the whisky can hold its head up high.

[8] Extremely famous writer on beer and whisky, not the MJ you probably first thought of.

Nose   Nutty, with waxy hints (floor polish); citrus.

Taste   Dried fruits, vanilla, oak – quite a light, refreshing body.

Finish   Citrus, mint and tobacco smoke.

Verdict ....

....

11

Producer	Adnams
Distillery	Copper House, Southwold, Suffolk, England
Visitor Centre	Yes
Availability	Likely specialists and distillery
Price	To be announced

Adnams

Adnams

Let's take a bit of a gamble. In the previous *101 Whiskies* I speculated that the whisky from St George's in Roudham, Norfolk, was going to work out just fine. And it did.

By the time this edition has been around for under a year, the next English whisky should be about to reach the shelves. I predict that it, too, will be excellent. It's definitely one to look out for.

This will have been produced by Adnams, a family-owned firm of traditional ale brewers in the thoroughly agreeable seaside town of Southwold in Suffolk, famous for its very fine pier, among other things. There is a delightfully eccentric collection of amusement machines there, created by the oddball inventor Tim Hunkin, that would justify a trip to Southwold all on their own. However, you should really visit the brewery and distillery, and marvel at the innovation and fresh thinking that is English whisky.

Inspired by the American craft-distilling revival, Adnams ordered pot and column stills from the renowned German makers Carl GmbH and had their Copper House Distillery up and running in late 2010. It's already noted for energy efficiency (a growing concern for the distilling industry) and making some fine products. They offer two excellent types of gin and vodka and various liqueurs (try the zesty Limoncello); and these have been picking up various awards and plaudits. The brewery is renowned for the quality of its beers and the distillery has been well planned – there's every reason, therefore, to look forward with optimism to the arrival of the whisky, which they have announced they expect to be bottling in November 2013.

I anticipate this with enormous enthusiasm and salute their energy, optimism and entrepreneurial spirit. Based on tasting their superb ales, splendid Copper House and First Rate Gin and their North Cove Oak Aged Vodka (be aware that these use a somewhat different production regime), I shall certainly be booking a trip to the seaside in late 2013 and anticipating the first taste with enormous relish.

What's more, they're already offering distillery tours and have an excellent restaurant, cook shop and off-licence just up the road.

Apparently a rye whisky is also under consideration. The thought of that is almost too exciting to bear!

Verdict

12

Producer	**St George's Chapter 6**
Distillery	The English Whisky Co.
	St George's, Roudham, Norfolk, England
Visitor Centre	Yes
Availability	Limited specialists and distillery
Price	▢▢

www.englishwhisky.co.uk

St George's
Chapter 6

I took a small gamble in *101 Whiskies* and listed St George's, despite the fact that it wasn't at that time legally whisky. 'This is the kind of thing that brings much-needed variety, excitement and interest to the whisky scene,' I wrote; suggesting that, 'You can buy with confidence.'

Fortunately, all turned out well. Truth to tell, it wasn't that big a gamble, improbable as English whisky may sound. The distillery was well financed, properly run and committed to getting things right first time – which was just as well given the incredible media attention it created. In fact, their only mistake was to run out of whisky, such was the resulting demand.

Well, things have calmed down now and we can see that St George's is more than a novelty. They style their releases 'chapters', reflecting the continued evolution of the distillery and the product.

Naturally, bowing to popular pressure and reflecting the fact that their first distiller came from Islay, they do a peated style (Chapters 9 and 11) but I'm going to suggest that you leave the smoky stuff to the Scots and try Chapter 6.

Two reasons: firstly, it seems to me that this shows the distillery character rather more clearly, thus enabling you better to judge the underlying spirit; and secondly, I'm not all that fond of a peat-drenched dram anyway. But it's there if you want it, which many of you do.

As the historians will recall, there were English whisky distilleries up until the arrival of the twentieth century. Until Adnams comes of age, we have just St George's flying the flag, alongside the tiny Hicks & Healey Cornish Single Malt which, at 7 years of age, actually started life before the Roudham pioneers. Unfortunately, that costs a staggering £210 for the equivalent of a standard bottle (although you do get two glasses with it). That's close to the price of a six-pack of St George's.

No prizes then for guessing why I suggest you try this one.

Nose Voluptuous, rounded and smooth. Warm vanilla and hot toffee sauce.

Taste All over vanilla and wood impact. Lively but not aggressive.

Finish A surprise bite on the finish; a late blast of spice and pepper. The youthful exuberance revealed at last!

Verdict ....

....

13

Producer
Distillery
Visitor Centre
Availability
Price

Teerenpeli
Single Malt 8 Years Old
Teerenpeli
Teerenpeli, Lahti, Finland
Yes
Limited specialists and distillery
▢▢▢▢

50cl ℮

43% vol

www.teerenpeli.com

Teerenpeli

Single Malt 8 Years Old

I probably shouldn't have been surprised to turn a corner at the 2011 London Whisky Live (great show, by the way, try to get a ticket) to see 8-year-old Finnish whisky, but I was. Not so much surprised that someone was making whisky in Finland, but because it was so mature and so very good. The packaging was also pretty sophisticated, suggesting that they're not playing at this.

It just goes to show that whisky can continue to astonish and delight all of us. I then discovered that Teerenpeli have been making whisky since 2002; although, until very recently, they were only selling it at their restaurant and distillery in Lahti, which is about 60 miles north-east of Helsinki.

They use locally grown barley, which is lightly peated, and mature their spirit in both sherry and bourbon casks, which apparently they source from the Speyside Cooperage. Good wood is, as we know, absolutely vital to good whisky, so full marks to them for that.

Sadly, it isn't exactly easy to find. Early production was very limited and, even today, they are only making 15,000 litres annually (by way of comparison, a small Scottish distillery such as Kilchoman will make around six and a half times that). However, if you want to be sure of getting some, you can commission your own cask. But then, of course, you have to wait throughout the maturation period.

My one Finnish friend tells me that the name Teerenpeli means 'flirtation' or 'dalliance'. Well, there is nothing flirtatious about this whisky – it is seriously well-made, well-packaged and well worth seeking out. Their website talks about maturation periods of up to 20 years, a further demonstration of their serious intent and professional approach.

You can visit the distillery and associated brewery and eat at the restaurant. How very agreeable! I really have to get there and find out more.

P.S. They are so proud of the packaging, they insisted we use this picture.

Nose   Pleasantly earthy; then floral.

Taste   Mouth filling and creamy; nuts, vanilla and fruit salad. Opens nicely with water.

Finish   Clean and fresh with long-lasting spices.

Verdict ....

....

14

Producer
Distillery

Visitor Centre
Availability
Price

Armorik Classic
Warenghem
Warenghem, Lannion, Brittany, France
Yes (summer months)
Limited specialists and distillery

www.distillerie-warenghem.com

Armorik Classic

Tempted as I am to make some (lame) Inspector Clouseau jokes, French whisky still comes as a bit of a shock. Unless you've been paying attention.

For, in the land of Armagnac, Calvados and Cognac, there are, at the last count, seven small whisky distilleries, with a cluster in the Brittany region. So we'd better start taking this seriously. They do: these are some of the most whisky-minded people you can find.

Output is small, however, and availability outside France pretty restricted. So I've taken just this one producer as an example of how whisky is spreading around the world. It may seem insignificant but the hegemony of the major-producing nations is being broken down, still by still.

Warenghem was established in 1900 to make liqueurs, but they were the pioneers of French whisky in 1987, graduating to single malt by 1994. It's actually a significant enterprise, employing around fifteen people and also producing beer and cider, various liqueurs and kirsch.

Today they offer both blended and single malt styles in a variety of expressions, which they call 'Breton Whisky' – the rugged Brittany countryside considers itself a Celtic nation and there is a vigorous nationalist movement that is both cultural and political.

In the context of Brittany's cultural and linguistic links to other Celtic communities, the distillation of whisky makes perfect sense as an expression of national or regional identity. This is whisky as Robert Burns, Aeneas MacDonald or Neil Gunn would recognise it, imbued with a deeper metaphorical significance and meaning than a mere drink. In the face of such profound considerations, today's talk of whisky as a 'financial investment' is revealed as callow and tawdry. Producers such as this remind us of whisky's artisanal roots and its spiritual significance. Even if their whisky is hard to find, true whisky lovers should salute them.

For more information on the various French whisky distilleries, visit www.frenchwhisky.com where there is also an online shop.

Nose   Leaf mould, like a forest after rain; dried fruits.

Taste   Wood smoke; slightly vegetal; citrus notes develop, as well as baked apples with cloves.

Finish   Quite abrupt. C'est tout.

Verdict

15

Blaue Maus

Producer	Fleischmann
Distillery	Blaue Maus, Eggolsheim-Neuses, Germany
Visitor Centre	Yes
Availability	Limited specialists and distillery
Price	

www.fleischmann-whisky.de

Blaue Maus

This is Germany's number one single malt whisky distillery and, yes, there is a number two – and many others, in fact. As many as thirty distilleries are now making German whisky. But Fleischmann's Blaue Maus distillery is the original and the genuine article, so far as product quality goes.

Its origins can be traced to 1983 but the owners weren't satisfied with the quality and nothing appeared on the open market until Glen Mouse (now Blaue Maus) was released in 1986. From there, the whisky and the wacky names have proliferated – today they produce whiskies whose names translate as Blue Mouse, Green Dog, Black Pirate and Old Driving (I've no idea either), among others. There's also one called Krottentaler, which they translate as 'Glen of the caves = Valley of the Rebel'. Makes you want to try it, doesn't it?

However, it's not all comedy names (who said the Germans have no sense of humour?) because they even offer a single cask grain whisky under the Austrasier label. If you doubt the serious intent, you can get a good impression of the distillery off the website (if you look hard enough there's a button which offers a range of different languages) and you'll realise that, though small and quirky, it's a perfectly serious operation.

In fact, it dates from 2006 when a distillery dedicated to whisky was opened. But some idiosyncratic details remain: everything is bottled as a single cask, so if you do track down a bottle (and you should try) it will be different to the one I drank and, unusually, the casks are all new wood (German oak, of course).

At the start of operations, no one told the then-owner Robert Fleischmann that he should char the inside of the barrels, so it never occurred to him to do so. Now that forms part of the distillery's distinctive and idiosyncratic style, and is an essential component to the Blaue Maus taste.

Experimentation, innovation and a sense of mischief – what's not to like? Along with the Bavarian Slyrs Distillery, Blaue Maus should make us think again about what whisky is and could be.

Nose   Roses, peaches and cream.

Taste   Ripe bananas, honey and apricot jam.

Finish   Not long, but satisfyingly warm.

Verdict

16

Producer Slyrs
Distillery Slyrs, Schliersee-Neuhaus, Germany

Visitor Centre Yes
Availability Limited specialists and distillery
Price ◻◻◻

Slyrs

www.slyrs.de

Slyrs

Much as I'd like to pretend that I've visited this Bavarian distillery so can tell you all about it, that wouldn't be true. In fact, I saw a bottle in an Edinburgh off-licence, bought it, liked it and looked up the rest in reference books (thank you Dave Broom and Ingvar Ronde) and on the web.

So, apart from the fact that I've tried it and you almost certainly haven't, with a few minutes' research you could know as much about it as I do. No need to bother, though, just read the rest of this entry for enlightenment.

Like so many small, new 'world' distilleries, when this was started in 1928 it was to make brandy and fruit spirits. Whisky's new-found fashionability persuaded the owners to try producing whisky in 1999, making them one of the founding fathers of European whisky making. By 2007, it was enough of a success for them to install their own custom-designed pot stills. Further expansion in 2009–10 means that they now produce around 60,000 bottles annually, so this is not exactly a boutique operation any more. Their whisky is highly regarded and this would stand up well in a blind tasting against some top-class competition. It might even give one or two very well-established names a fright.

This release was non-chill filtered and I understand that the distillery have retained quantities of earlier distillations for further maturation and a phased release, so you could well find an older expression, or possibly the cask strength Raritas Diaboli. Reputedly, we may see a 12-year-old in 2015, which is exciting news.

There are now around thirty different German whiskies. Sadly, we only have room here for two of the best of them but the very number of them is further proof, if proof were needed, of whisky's incredible ability to develop and evolve in the most surprising of places.

Some tasting notes on the web refer to 'rubber wellies'. I can't even begin to imagine what they've been up to.

Nose   Fragrant vanilla essence and wood notes. Hay-like.

Taste   Loads more of that vanilla; some citrus notes detectable underneath, with honey hints. Medium bodied.

Finish   Disperses fairly quickly.

Verdict ....

17

Amrut Single Malt

Producer	Amrut Distilleries Ltd
Distillery	Amrut, Bangalore, India
Visitor Centre	Yes
Availability	Specialists
Price	☐☐

www.amrutwhisky.co.uk

Amrut
Single Malt

You do realise, don't you, that the four most popular domestic Indian whiskies sell more in India than all the Scotch in all of the world put together? You didn't?

That may be because it can't be sold as 'whisky' in the EU – it is made from molasses and is, therefore, considered to be rum. Quite right, too. Anyway, with names like Bagpiper, people in Britain are inclined to laugh at Indian whisky and forget that we Brits set up the industry there in the first place.

But 50 years ago we sneered at Japanese whisky and look where that is today. So, when we see signs of an emergent affluent middle class changing things in India and legitimate Indian single malt arriving on European shores, we might want to pay attention. You should certainly pay attention to Amrut.

This relatively small Indian distiller was established in 1948 but only began selling what we would recognise as whisky to the UK in 2004. At first, progress was patchy. But the product has been reformulated; a number of highly successful special editions have been launched and there is a core range of five products now available year round in Western Europe, Scandinavia, three provinces in Canada and in the United States.

The 'entry level' single malt, if you will, is this 46% abv style made from Indian barley and, as it says rather poetically on the label, 'nurtured by waters flowing from the Great Himalayas'. Their whiskies have won any number of different awards in a very short time and they were *Whisky Magazine*'s 2011 Distiller of the Year in the Rest of the World category.

Because of the climate over there we're unlikely ever to see very old Indian whiskies (while Scotch can mature for 50 years or more), but perhaps in 50 years' time we'll look at Indian whisky with rather more respect. Or perhaps, quite possibly, it won't take that long. Remember, you read it here first.

Nose   Marzipan, toffee and molasses (sorry!).

Taste   Agreeably spicy, this evolves into a sweeter middle, reminiscent of digestive biscuits and some hints of ripe plums and peaches.

Finish   A gentle, medium-length finish, with fruit and spices again to the fore.

Verdict ....

....

18

Producer
Distillery

Visitor Centre
Availability
Price

Connemara Peated Single Malt
Cooley Distillery PLC
Cooley, Riverstown, Co. Louth, Ireland
Yes – tours by appointment
Specialists

www.connemarawhiskey.com

Connemara

Peated Single Malt

Cooley Distillers spent a lot of time in recent years proudly proclaiming themselves 'the only Irish-owned Irish whiskey distillery', but sold out to Beam Inc. of the USA at the end of 2011 for $95 million. They are very much Ireland's third force, but nonetheless visible and noteworthy for all that. And in all the current excitement about the Irish revival, let's not forget that they built the first new distillery in Ireland in over 100 years.

Zigging where others choose to zag, I have never really got on board the peat-fuelled train, preferring my whisky rather subtler in taste. But there's no denying its popularity and as I'm not here to dictate what you should drink, but simply to suggest some ideas, if your palate tends to the smoky then, by all means, give this a go.

Even before you get this to your mouth it tells you that it's robust and full of character. Old distiller's trick: rub a little on your hands and then, cupping them together, smell them (as a rather nice bonus you look ever so confident and knowledgeable). The peat smoke comes roaring through, but – praise be – it's not as harsh as its opposite numbers on Islay. And, after that, it calms down: in fact, it's really quite smooth and a perfectly pleasant underlying sweetness emerges after a while. There is none of that assertively medicinal character – though, then again, you might actually like that.

However, if you do want a more intense flavour, this is also available at cask strength (57.9% abv and a Double Gold winner at the 2011 San Francisco World Spirits Competition) or as Turf Mór, a cask strength limited edition Small Batch Collection that has been created using very heavily peated malt (50 ppm for the smoke heads among you). I wasn't sure I could handle it, to be quite honest. You may also find a version at 12 Years Old.

But all praise to the folks at Cooley for this whiskey. As the smallest of the Irish distillers (though now with Beam behind them), they have had to be rather more creative and experimental in their whiskey making. This has paid off; sales are increasing in double digits and they've collected heaps of awards. It's all part of the general revival in Irish distilling and a very welcome development it is. Their whiskies are not expensive and they represent good, honest value. So try some.

Nose Fresh and relatively mild; smoke but also fruits and vanilla.

Taste Cut apples, honey, malted grains and buttered toast with lemon marmalade.

Finish More assertive than expected; possibly a slight rubber note at the end.

Verdict

19

Producer
Distillery

Visitor Centre
Availability
Price

Greenore Single Grain
Cooley Distillery PLC
Cooley, Riverstown, Co. Louth, Ireland
Yes – tours by appointment
Specialists

www.cooleywhiskey.com

Greenore
Single Grain

Given what they've achieved on their own, the prospect of what Cooley will bring us in years to come now that they have Beam's money behind them, is a tantalising one.

Yet they will have to come up with something pretty interesting and different to match this. This is Single Grain Irish Whiskey – something rarer than a sighting of leprechauns in Berkeley Square. In fact, this is currently the only Irish Single Grain that you can buy, which more or less guaranteed its inclusion here.

Until relatively recently, grain whiskey (or whisky) was the industry's dirty little secret, generally held to be useful only for blending and there was a discreet silence maintained over its somewhat industrial production. And, of course, grain whiskey (or 'sham whisky' as the great Dublin distillers of the nineteenth century termed it) played a major role in the decline of Irish distilling, as they rejected blending outright as adulteration of their product.

But, as Compass Box have proved, it can actually be very enjoyable in its own right and it is enjoying a modest burst of appreciation from thoughtful drinkers. Irish grain was first offered by Cooley as a 15-year-old version. It was showered with awards and was quickly followed by a limited edition 18-year-old, also highly praised; and now – at a slightly more accessible price point – comes this 8-year-old. In 2010 *Whisky Magazine* declared it to be the World's Best Single Grain.

Greenore is distilled from maize, with a small amount of malt used to start fermentation. It's then matured in former bourbon casks, so as not to overwhelm the relatively delicate flavour, and each year a few casks will be hand-picked by Cooley's Master Blender. There will never be huge amounts of this whiskey available but there will be small batches released at varying ages over the next few years.

My only slight criticism of this is that I would have liked to have seen it released at 46% abv like its older counterparts. In fact, is it too much to hope that we might see this at cask strength? There would be nothing 'sham' about that!

Nose   Sweet and immediately appealing; vanilla and pears.

Taste   Lighter bodied than some, but clean, buttery and refreshing.

Finish   Gone fairly quickly with a whiff of oak.

Verdict

20

Producer
Distillery
Visitor Centre

Availability
Price

Jameson Gold Reserve
Irish Distillers Ltd
Midleton, Cork, Ireland
Two – Old Jameson Distillery in Dublin
and Midleton Distillery in Cork
Specialists and better supermarkets
◻◻◻

www.jamesonwhiskey.com

Jameson

Gold Reserve

You can find several expressions of Jameson in the UK (although sadly not the remarkable Black Barrel which is reserved for the USA at the time of writing). Jameson is – justifiably – the best-selling Irish whiskey in the world, but you might want to consider taking a couple of steps up from the standard bottling to get it at its best. You can do better than Jimmy McNulty.

You can choose from Jameson (the standard); Select Reserve; 12 Year Old Special Reserve; Gold Reserve; 18 Year Old Limited Reserve (recommended in the last edition); Signature Reserve (if you use duty free shops); or Rarest Vintage Reserve. Let's try the Gold Reserve.

They all come from Irish Distillers Ltd's giant operation at Midleton, near Cork, which in December 2012 announced a €100 million expansion, this on top of a further €100 million investment in a new whiskey maturation facility in Dungourney near Midleton. How come?

Well, the distillers say this is their twenty-third consecutive year of growth and certainly Irish whiskey in general and Jameson in particular has been growing remarkably fast in the USA, its largest market by some distance. At the same time, they expect to reduce energy consumption by 33% and water usage by 20% per litre of alcohol produced. Sustainability will be a hugely important topic to the whole distilling industry over the next few years, so expect to see more announcements of this type.

At around £50 this is a first-class buy. Though no age is declared, the whiskey in Gold Reserve is 13–14 years old and very, very smooth and deliciously mouth coating. The full, oily character from the Irish pot still component of the blend comes to the fore; I'd like to see this offered at 43% abv or 46% abv, but it's rich, sumptuous and creamy all the same.

Note: if you do visit the Dublin or Midleton visitor centres you won't actually see an operating distillery but a heritage centre based around the originals. Close, but no cigar.

Nose   Honeyed sweetness followed by oak and spice.

Taste   Buttery; very, very smooth. Some sherry-wood character, fruit cake and Madeira wine. Mint and liquorice notes.

Finish   Holds together for a complex spice finale.

Verdict ....

....

21

Producer
Distillery

Visitor Centre
Availability
Price

Locke's 8 Year Old
Cooley Distillery PLC
Cooley, Riverstown, Co. Louth,
Ireland
Yes – tours by appointment
Specialists
◻◻

www.cooleywhiskey.com – but, sadly, no information on Locke's at time of writing

Locke's

8 Year Old

First established in 1987 in a converted potato alcohol plant, Cooley deserve the gratitude of all whiskey lovers for their reopening of the old Kilbeggan distillery and the company have also been active in saving some of the grand old names of Irish distilling, such as Tyrconnell. You could even argue that, without their influence, brands such as Redbreast and Green Spot would have been swept away by the corporate tide of 'progress', though I daresay the people who now promote those very brands so energetically would strenuously deny it.

Anyway, the name of Locke's is a hallowed one in Irish distilling. The family ran the Kilbeggan distillery (established in 1757, and thus one of the oldest, if not *the* oldest distillery in the world) from 1843 until its eventual closure in 1957. The whiskey in this bottle will, of course, have been distilled at Cooley, but there are plans in due course to switch production to Kilbeggan as the restoration allows. That will be a truly historic day and cause for celebration.

Locke's is a regular and justified award winner at the International Wine & Spirit Competition (most recently, Gold Best in Class). Connoisseurs applaud its creamy texture and fine balance, which is achieved through a mixture of peated and non-peated malts.

At a typical UK retail price of around £30, it's an affordable, well-made and easy-to-drink example of the Irish single malt whiskey style that is enjoying a justifiable revival.

Nose	Slightly dusty with aromas of freshly baked spice cake; then honey and spices. Citrus hints.
Taste	Mouth filling and warm; very smooth. Cereal notes and toffee; bread and honey followed by Simnel cake.
Finish	An extended burst of chewy caramel, with spiced orange making a final bow.

Verdict

22

Midleton Barry Crockett Legacy

Producer	Irish Distillers Ltd
Distillery	Midleton, Cork, Ireland
Visitor Centre	Two – Old Jameson Distillery in Dublin and Midleton Distillery in Cork
Availability	Limited specialists
Price	

www.jamesonwhiskey.com

Midleton
Barry Crockett Legacy

It must be slightly alarming having a whiskey named after you, rather like one of those 'lifetime achievement' awards they give to actors who have never quite lifted an Oscar; should have done but probably never will now that they're in their dotage.

However, Barry Crockett seemed pretty well last time I met him. As he delights in telling you, he was actually born in a cottage in the grounds of the distillery (well before the 'new' one was built) and took over from his father as Master Distiller in 1981. So he's as entitled as anyone to a legacy and a very fine one this is.

It's part of the new series of pot still Irish whiskies released by Irish Distillers (see also Powers and Redbreast) as their serious, albeit belated, commitment to the traditional style of distilling, in this case using exclusively American bourbon barrels for maturation. Very unusually, they also employ some brand new American oak barrels – this would normally be thought to overwhelm the spirit but, used in moderation, it does dramatically enhance the creamy mouth feel and spicy character.

Naturally, this has been released at 46% abv (Green Spot, which I recommended in *101 Whiskies to Try Before You Die*, has stayed at 40% abv – missed opportunity, chaps) and it is non-chill filtered. There is no age declaration but they say the whiskies are between 10 and 22 years of age.

I suppose it is the age and the nice but essentially redundant wooden box that the bottle comes in, which accounts for the price; my one concern about this whiskey. It's close to £150. Quantities are limited, so it is rather special, but still.

However, we're arguing about a man's legacy here so let's not be churlish – buy it and celebrate one of the great names in world distilling.

Nose   Pears, vanilla and some citrus hints. A slice of bread and honey.

Taste   More delicate than the Powers stablemate, but complex, spicy, peppery and with kiwi fruits and ripe melon.

Finish   Satisfyingly long and consistent, tailing off with some oaky suggestions.

Verdict

23

Producer	Irish Distillers Ltd
Distillery	Midleton, Cork, Ireland
Visitor Centre	Two – Old Jameson Distillery in Dublin and Midleton Distillery in Cork
Availability	Limited specialists
Price	

Powers John's Lane Release

www.powerswhiskey.com

Powers

John's Lane Release

The old John's Lane distillery was in Dublin and, in the days when Irish distilling ruled the world, was one of the largest pot still distilleries in the world. However, the Irish distilling industry contrived to get themselves into a bit of a mess (massive over-simplification there) and any number of outside factors conspired to make their life even harder. Scotch whisky pretty much took over world markets.

Eventually, and tragically, all the great Dublin distilleries closed and the majority of Irish whiskey production was concentrated in one new distillery at Midleton, near Cork, which opened in 1975. With a variety of shapes and styles of stills they can and do make an astonishing range of spirits there. It took a while, but it's been a great success and, as part of Pernod Ricard, has been expanded very successfully. Their lead brand Jameson has been growing and growing and, with the increased confidence and consumer interest in Irish whiskey, they have felt able to bring back some of the older styles. This Powers is 12 years old and bottled at 46% abv.

So, like the cask-strength Redbreast (number 24), this is a true pot still whiskey. And what an impact it has had! This whiskey lit up international forums and blogs and was praised to the skies. It wasn't just that Irish Distillers had finally acknowledged their birthright, nor that they launched this with three other related whiskies, it was the sheer quality of the product that excited people. How had something this good fallen out of favour? Why had the world remained in ignorance for so long?

Well, whatever the answer, be in no doubt that with this and its stablemates, Irish whiskey is back with a vengeance. If Irish Distillers put the same kind of imagination, resource and talent into this that they have done with Jamesons, then they are on to a winner and we are all the better for it.

Nose   Treacle tart, leather and tobacco (like the inside of a classic old sports car) and spices.

Taste   Very full bodied and oily, with spices, vanilla, honey and dried fruit.

Finish   Lingers nicely to a long, mellow conclusion, suggesting coffee and chocolate orange.

Verdict
....

....

24

Producer
Distillery
Visitor Centre

Availability
Price

Redbreast Cask Strength
Irish Distillers Ltd
Midleton, Cork, Ireland
Two – Old Jameson Distillery in Dublin
and Midleton Distillery in Cork
Specialists and better supermarkets

www.irishdistillers.ie

Redbreast
Cask Strength

In the last book I lavished praise on the 'standard' 12-year-old Redbreast, one of the great Irish pot still whiskies. Since then, things have been getting better and better for Irish whiskey as Irish Distillers' parent, the giant Pernod Ricard group, have poured resources into the category as a whole and Midleton Distillery in particular.

The distillery has been expanded, especially with the building of new warehouses, and there have been a number of exciting releases, particularly this cask strength version of Redbreast (57.7% abv for the initial batch).

Irish pot still whiskey differs from Scotch single malt in that it is made from a mixture of malted and unmalted barley and is distilled three times (twice is the norm in Scotland, with some exceptions). Up until the early 1900s, this was the best-selling whiskey style in the world, but the Irish industry declined very rapidly and has only recently begun to recover.

Regarded by many as the definitive expression of traditional pot still Irish whiskey, Redbreast dates back to 1903 when Jameson entered into an agreement with the Gilbeys Wines & Spirits Import Company to supply them with new make spirit from their Bow Street Distillery in Dublin (now sadly operating only as a heritage centre). The custom of that era was that distilleries sold bulk whiskey to 'bonders' who, being in the business of importing fortified wines such as sherry and Port, had ample supplies of empty casks in which to mature new make whiskeys under bond.

Bringing this back in a non-chill filtered, cask-strength style was a stroke of genius and proves that at least some distillers listen to their customers. It costs more than the standard version, of course, but it's worth every penny. A masterpiece.

Nose   Big fruit with loads of oak character.

Taste   The signature sherry cask note of Christmas cake and dried fruit blows you away, but is followed by more delicate spice and bitter oranges, studded with cloves.

Finish   Warm, spicy, mouth coating; everything you hoped for when you read the label!

Verdict ....

....

25

Producer

Distillery
Visitor Centre

Availability
Price

■ ■
Tullamore Dew 12 Years Old
Irish Distillers Ltd for William Grant
& Sons
Midleton, Cork, Ireland
Heritage centre at the original
Tullamore distillery, Tullamore
Specialists and some supermarkets
□□

www.tullamoredew.com

Tullamore Dew

12 Years Old

The observant reader will have noted that there are few more Irish whiskies in this book than the previous edition. Tullamore Dew is part of the renaissance in Irish distilling and, in fact, claims to be the fastest-growing brand in that market. So, hats off to William Grant & Sons who acquired this famous old brand in July 2010 and have been investing heavily in it ever since.

Given what they have done in single malt and blended Scotch one imagines that their rivals have been watching with a mixture of trepidation and anxiety, tempered by the thought that anything which promotes Irish whiskey must be good for all. Or so they will be hoping.

The original Tullamore distillery, now a heritage centre, was founded as far back as 1829. However, in 1862, one Daniel Edmond Williams joined the distillery as a young man. Eventually he became General Manager, employed his initials (DEW) on a brand and by 1903 his family were majority owners. But sadly, Tullamore suffered the same vicissitudes as the rest of the industry and by the 1960s the distillery had closed and production transferred to Irish Distiller at Midleton. Ownership changed in 1994 and then again in 2010. At the time of writing, Grants had just announced at €35m scheme for a new distillery at Tullamore.

This standard style is hardly the most demanding whiskey you'll ever encounter, though it's not to be underestimated. Fans of Lisbeth Salander (The Girl with the Dragon Tattoo) will recall that she found Lagavulin "a mortal enemy" but was partial to Tullamore Dew.

Whether you consider a near-psychopathic computer hacker with a penchant for kinky violence a role model for your drinking I leave to your better judgement – but personally I wouldn't mess with her. "Give every man his Dew" as they used to say.

You might want to spend a few more pounds and trade up to the 12 year old version. There's more pot still and malt whiskey in there and greater complexity from the additional aging.

Nose   Bread and butter with lemon curd.

Taste   Toast, vanilla, sweet spices, lemon rind and nuts.

Finish   Surprisingly long and gentle with spicy back notes.

Verdict

26

Producer
Distillery

Visitor Centre
Availability
Price

Writers Tears
Writers Tears Whiskey Co.
Unofficially, it has to be Midleton,
Cork, Ireland, but no one is saying
No
Specialists

www.writerstears.com

Writers Tears

How could I NOT include a whiskey called Writers Tears (even if they have missed out the apostrophe)? After all, the pages of this book are stained with the tears of joy, frustration, exhilaration and infuriation that come with writing a whisky book. What to include? What to leave out? How to write when severely under the influence of a powerful drug? (Night Nurse, in this case.)

Anyway, that's enough about me. After the capture of Cooley by the forces of global capitalism, this is the last independent Irish whiskey company. But, like Compass Box (Scotland) and McLain & Kyne (USA) they aren't distillers but independent bottlers – 'whiskey designers', if you will.

Writers Tears Whiskey Company is the brainchild of Bernard and Rosemary Walsh, who are also behind the Hot Irishman business. The whiskey itself is an unusual, possibly unique, vatting of pure pot still and Irish single malt and, though no one will say on the record, it almost certainly comes from Irish Distillers' operation at Midleton. The company claim it's a recreation of a style that was around a century or so ago.

I don't suppose we'll ever know if that's really the case since, tragically, so much Irish whiskey history has been lost. But it makes for an agreeable link to James Joyce, Samuel Beckett, Oscar Wilde and other great Irish writers who appear on the website (where you'll find some great stories about writers and their haunts). Whiskey and great writing do seem to go together.

Frankly, I wouldn't really care if some of this was made up. The whiskey carries all before it. With products like this it's incredible that the Irish got into the mess that they did and not at all surprising that they're on a roll today.

If this wasn't around I would have had to write about the Feckin' Irish[9]. And nobody wants that.

[9] I'm not being rude; it's a whiskey. Apparently.

Nose   Light and delicate notes of honey, pears, lemon zest and ginger.

Taste   Vanilla, honey and crème brûlée; mixed spice with ginger to the fore; drinks stronger than its 40% abv strength.

Finish Rich and warming as the spice notes roll on to an extended finish.

Verdict ....

27

Producer	Akashi White Oak
Distillery	Eigashima Shuzo
	White Oak, Akashi-shi, Honshu,
	Japan
Visitor Centre	Yes
Availability	Limited specialists
Price	◻◻

Akashi

White Oak

A simple cardboard box with a paper label stuck on it and a cough syrup bottle. At the equivalent of £35 a bottle, how do they get away with it? Especially when they're mainly sake distillers.

Because, as you will discover when you try it, it's really very agreeable, well-made stuff.

In fairness, whisky is supposed to have been made here since 1919 so there is a track record, even if the whisky side of the operation is small and not yet well known, other than among hard-core enthusiasts. Currently, the distilling takes place in a purpose-built plant dating from 1984. Most of that whisky went into a White Oak blend sold only in Japan but, observing the single malt boom and the growing worldwide interest in Japanese whisky, Eigashima have been spreading their wings somewhat. This may well be one to watch.

Encouraged by the reaction to their first release of an 8-year-old single malt, Eigashima have signed a deal with the French whisky specialists Les Whiskies du Monde to bring 5- and 12-year-old single malts and this tasty blend to Europe. Rumour has it that there will also be a 14-year-old single malt sometime in 2012.

The availability of these whiskies outside Japan marks a further stage of development in an industry that is, rightly, growing in confidence and self-assurance. Japanese whisky has now moved out from under the shadow of the Scotch style, which it was initially modelled on and emulated for so long, to offer a distinctive take on distilling that all lovers of the cratur will welcome. Eigashima is not a large producer but its products offer yet more evidence of the infinite variety to be found in the world of whisky.

The company's website appears to be only available in Japanese. Hopefully with greater export success, they'll offer an English language version soon. I did manage to gather that there is a small museum at the distillery which is open to visitors. One day!

Nose   Honey, apples and wood.

Taste   Attractive ginger spice; more fruit notes, then developing a creamy sweetness.

Finish   Some smoke appears to add intrigue at the last.

Verdict

28

Producer	Chichibu
Distillery	Chichibu, Saitama, Japan
Visitor Centre	No
Availability	Limited specialists
Price	▉▉▉▉

Chichibu The First

Ichiro's Malt
CHICHIBU

Japanese Single Malt Whisky
THE FIRST
Distilled 2008   Bottled 2011

秩父

Bottle #   1 / 7400

Chichibu

The First

Here in the decadent West we tend to get rather excited about father and son distilling dynasties; we come over all respectful if they last more than two generations and revere companies which have remained in family hands for any longer than that.

So meet a man – Ichiro Akuto – who is the twenty-first generation of his family in the drinks industry. Unfortunately, the family business went bankrupt, but Akuto ended up buying up the old stocks of whisky with the eventual aim of building his own distillery.

Now he has done it. Construction of his Chichibu distillery commenced in spring 2007; the first distillery built in Japan since Hakushu in the 1970s. Distilling licences were granted and production began in February 2008. And now the whisky is ready.

Fittingly, it is called 'The First'. There are fewer than 4,000 bottles to go round and most of those will be eagerly snapped up by collectors and smart whisky bars, ever anxious to maintain their cutting edge. But a Norwich-based importer, Number One Drinks Company, has the European agency and, as further stocks are released, they will be bringing them to our shores. Look out for them and, if you see a bottle, grab it quick. Never mind the price tag; if you hesitate, it will be gone.

Applaud this initiative! The time has long passed since we could look down with patronising disdain on Japanese whisky. Enthusiasts now recognise its outstanding quality and smaller, craft-based operations such as Chichibu offer variety, intensity and a personal approach far removed from the industry's corporate giants.

Chichibu may use malt from Germany and England, a British mill, and stills specifically manufactured in Scotland, but the distilling itself is approached with a distinctively Japanese sensibility that is apparent from the first taste.

Take note now: although small, this is going to become an increasingly important player in the European scene for Japanese whiskies. Expect to see this name on many, many award citations in the near future.

Nose   Mild Thai curry spices; nutty with some sweetness emerging.

Taste   Well rounded and assertive (at 61.8% abv cask strength); sweetness emerges with water, along with oak and soft fruits.

Finish   Pleasant, if slightly short.

Verdict ....

....

29

Producer
Distillery

Visitor Centre
Availability
Price

| • |

Miyagikyo 10 Years Old
The Nikka Whisky Distilling Co. Ltd
Miyagikyo, near Sendai, Honshu,
Japan
Yes
Specialists and distillery
□□□

www.nikkawhisky.eu

Miyagikyo

10 Years Old

Miyagikyo was founded as recently as 1969 by Masataka Taketsuru, founder of Nikka and revered as instrumental in the creation and development of Japanese whisky. Though Nikka are Japan's second distiller after Suntory, some interesting whiskies are emerging from Miyagikyo, not least their Coffey Grain – single malt produced in a continuous still. They would not be permitted to do this in Scotland and call the spirit 'single malt' – perhaps this is the difference in entrepreneurial attitude between our two countries. It's certainly created a lot of interest among enthusiasts.

Ironic, isn't it, that an industry which started by imitating Scotch (not terribly well at first) has now developed the confidence and standing to follow its own path; to represent a specifically Japanese ethos and philosophy; and to innovate where the instinct in Scotland is now to proscribe and constrain?

Given that Nikka own the Ben Nevis distillery in Fort William which once housed a continuous still, one might hazard a guess that they could be tempted … but let us not pursue that seditious train of thought. That way madness lies, or lawyers' letters anyway.

So the selection here is somewhat less controversial. Their Miyagikyo single malt is stylistically at some distance from the whisky from Yoichi (which I listed in the first *101 Whiskies*). Where that is full and peaty, this provides more delicacy and subtlety, though with no loss of complexity.

Three versions are fairly easily found in European markets (10, 12 and 15 Years Old) but the older versions jump up somewhat in price, so it may be an idea to start with the 10 Years Old, unless particularly convinced that you'll love them (or perhaps you can convince an indulgent friend to buy all three and then you can compare them).

Incidentally, at one time export bottlings of Miyagikyo were known as Sendai so you may, if fortunate, come across some very old stock, probably at a whisky auction. If no one else realises what's going on, casually nod at the auctioneer and try not to look too excited.

Nose   Cereal hints, some floral notes but quite subtle.

Taste   Great balance; banana and pineapple notes; chocolate and oak in the background.

Finish   Restrained, elegant and holds together well.

Verdict ....

....

30

Producer
Distillery

Visitor Centre
Availability
Price

Nikka From the Barrel
The Nikka Whisky Distilling Co. Ltd
Miyagikyo, near Sendai, Honshu,
Japan and Yoichi, near Sapporo,
southern Hokkaido, Japan
Yes – at Miyagikyo and Yoichi distilleries
Specialists and distillery

NIKKA WHISKY
FROM
THE BARREL
alc. 51.4°

ウイスキー
原材料 モルト・グレーン
●容量 500ml ●アルコール分 51.4%
製造者 ニッカウキスキー株式会社 6
東京都港区南青山5-4-31 06E22D

Nikka

From the Barrel

If you've never tried a Japanese whisky, you could do a lot worse than start here. For one thing, Nikka make whisky that is still strongly influenced by the Scottish traditions absorbed and upheld by their founder Masataka Taketsuru so, on first impression, the whisky may seem strangely familiar.

Then this unassuming little bottle, with its modest screw cap, starts to surprise and delight you. The contents are smooth and seductive, well-mannered and beguiling. The curiously recognisable flavours begin to evolve in unexpected directions; as you explore the taste it will grow on you, being at once comfortingly seated within your normal drinking repertoire (assuming you drink Scotch, that is) and yet strangely different – as if an old friend had moved abroad and adopted the cultural norms of his new home.

With products such as this, Japanese whisky is making inroads into our drinking. Whisky aficionados may have tried this and moved on in their quest for something more exotic but its quality cannot be denied. The standard bottle price equivalent is around £40 which, for a 51.4% abv product, isn't at all unreasonable.

The whisky is unaged but is certainly not some raw, callow stripling. There is plenty of maturity here and the impact of the first-fill casks and some inspired blending is clear. It's undoubtedly one to try blind on your whisky-loving friends to see what they make of it.

Nikka From the Barrel offers an accessible first taste that will have you looking for more. And, if you like it, you can move on to the single malts from Miyagikyo and Yoichi distilleries, both fairly easily found in a 10-year-old expression, or Nikka's intriguing Coffey Grain. The two Nikka distilleries produce fine, award-winning whiskies and are highly regarded. As Nikka themselves say, their whisky 'dares. It captures the senses. It imposes its own style.'

Nose   Vanilla, fruit cake and wood smoke.

Taste   Notably rounded and smooth, even when neat; with water a more floral character emerges, and some lighter fruit and spice notes can be detected.

Finish A sustained and consistent balancing act.

Verdict

31

Producer
Distillery

Visitor Centre
Availability
Price

Nikka Taketsuru 21 Years Old
The Nikka Whisky Distilling Co. Ltd
Miyagikyo, near Sendai, Honshu,
Japan and Yoichi, near Sapporo,
southern Hokkaido, Japan
Yes – at Miyagikyo and Yoichi distilleries
Specialists and distillery
▢▢▢▢

www.nikkawhisky.eu

Nikka

Taketsuru 21 Years Old

Nikka call this 'pure malt', which would be outlawed in Scotland where it would be known as 'blended malt'. I call it a stunningly, stunningly good malt.

And it seems the world agrees, because this is a major flagship for Nikka, collecting prestigious awards as some of us do parking tickets. It takes its name from company founder Masataka Taketsuru who, in 1916, came to Scotland to study Applied Chemistry and Distilling. He worked briefly at both Hazelburn (when Campbeltown was flourishing) and at Longmorn; both experiences established a deep and abiding love of Scotland.

He returned with a Scottish wife and a burning determination to set up a Japanese industry that made 'real' whisky. His early work was with Suntory but, in 1934, he established the company that we know today as The Nikka Whisky Distilling Company at Yoichi. The Miyagikyo distillery is a comparative youngster, opening as recently as 1969, but it has at least one still (used for grain whisky) dating back to the nineteenth century.

Nikka's Taketsuru range celebrates the achievements of the founder and, with that legacy in mind, you can take a shrewd guess that the company are never going to use anything but their better whiskies to make up the different expressions. These are available at 12, 17 and 21 years of age. There is also a very limited quantity of a 35-year-old version, but this was intended solely for sale in Japan. I'll admit to never actually having even seen a bottle of this (and I've never tasted it, of course) but if I did I'd buy it on sight.

The pick here is the 21-year-old, as this whisky does seem to get better with age but, honestly, you wouldn't be disappointed in any of them. For some reason, Japanese whiskies have become a particular success in France. But don't let our good friends over the Channel have them all to themselves; buy a few bottles and let's try to encourage Nikka to make more delicious drams and send them to their spiritual home (and England).

Nose   Ripe plums, oak and coffee beans.

Taste   Spice, peel and orange marmalade.

Finish   Lasts and lasts as the complexity gently unravels.

Verdict

32

Producer
Distillery
Visitor Centre
Availability
Price

No. 1 Single Cask Bottlings
Number One Drinks Company
Various
No
Specialists
▢▢▢▢

www.one-drinks.com

No. 1
Single Cask Bottlings

What is this doing here, you might well ask. Especially since this Norwich-based company is actually an importer, rather than a distiller.

Well, they get this space because they represent an opportunity for the European consumer to obtain rare and unusual Japanese whiskies which, until they started importing them in 2006, simply weren't available. For that, they have done us all a great service and opened many eyes to the fantastic quality available from Japan. Today they have exclusive representation of some of these products, which are necessarily in short supply.

The company was founded by Marcin Miller, formerly of *Whisky Magazine* and his partner David Croll, who is based in Tokyo. Aware that many remarkable whiskies were difficult for enthusiasts to find outside Japan, they began by importing an initial shipment of award-winning single malts from the defunct Hanyu Distillery. Today, whiskies are sourced in Japan by David Croll and samples are assessed by a tasting panel prior to selection; casks are then purchased, bottled and shipped to Miller in the UK to be sold to specialist retailers and whisky bars.

Their range includes Karuizawa, exclusive to Number One Drinks in Europe as they have secured all the remaining stocks; Hanyu; Chichibu (see number 28); and their own-label cask bottlings. These are most attractively and dramatically packaged and have been universally well received.

It may interest, reassure or excite you to know that of the twelve Gold Medals awarded by the Malt Maniacs in 2010, four were for whiskies sourced by Number One Drinks (three from Karuizawa). Endorsements don't come much higher than that (except being listed here, of course).

Because stocks are limited, there's little point in recommending any one whisky. Instead, look out for their name on bottles of obscure Japanese whiskies – it's a guarantee of quality and commitment from people close to the ground and with a real enthusiasm for their work.

You will not be disappointed.

Verdict ....

....

33

Producer
Distillery

Visitor Centre
Availability
Price

●

Yamazaki Sherry Cask
(also Bourbon Barrel and Puncheon)
Suntory
Yamazaki, near Osaka, Honshu,
Japan
Yes
Specialists and distillery
□□□

www.theyamazaki.jp

Yamazaki

Sherry Cask (also Bourbon Barrel and Puncheon)

Three for the price of one here! Yamazaki is the original Japanese whisky distillery and a very fine one. Its aged expressions have won many fans and you can even find a 50-year-old Yamazaki (but don't try too hard, they're about £8,000 a bottle and will be all gone by the time you read this!).

The distillery has been a pioneer in introducing its whiskies to the European market, where it has had considerable success. Suntory also own Morrison Bowmore, so have a strong UK base, and they have introduced their 12-year-old 'standard' Yamazaki to supermarkets. Last time I looked, I could buy it in Perth. One in the eye for the Scots, then.

But this range is something different: essentially it's Yamazaki showing the effect of different cask maturation regimes. You can choose from a big, beefy and very dark whisky from a sherry cask (it's about twice the price of the others at around £125 – no idea why); a spicier dram from a bourbon barrel; or, unusually, the result of aging in a puncheon – that's a larger-than-normal 480 litre cask so the whisky takes longer to mature.

None of them offer any clue as to their age on the packaging, but all are bottled at a standard 48% abv, the idea being that you compare and contrast. Did that – I slightly preferred the sherry expression, though all three were very fine. It just goes to show that tastes vary and there's no definitive or 'right' answer. This range showcases beautifully the complexity and diversity of just one distillery – there's something here for everyone.

As a stunning range to introduce yourself to Japanese whisky, this works superbly well. They aren't exactly cheap but they are very, very good.

Nose   A sherried classic – dark fruits, cake and wood notes, where the Puncheon offered sweeter, bubblegum notes and the Bourbon salted nuts. Coffee and chocolate here also.

Taste   A very big whisky, reminiscent of Yamazaki's 18 Year Old. Prunes, sultanas and spice. If you like The Macallan or Glenfarclas, you might enjoy this.

Finish   Lingers delightfully, teasing you with the memory of a sherry monster.

Verdict ....

....

34

Producer Us Heit
Distillery Us Heit, Bolsward,
The Netherlands

Visitor Centre Yes
Availability Limited specialists and distillery
Price

Frysk Hynder

www.usheitdistillery.nl

Frysk Hynder

Late in 2011 I was giving a tasting of (Scotch) whisky to delegates from an international environment and recycling conference in Glasgow's splendid House for an Art Lover when a delegate from Frisia very kindly presented me with a miniature of Frysk Hynder. And my heart sank.

Fortunately, though, they were all called off to their dinner (tough work these recycling conferences) so I wasn't obliged to drink it and comment there and then. Which was very handy. For two reasons.

First of all, I didn't have to try to find something to say about a whisky that I knew nothing about in front of an eager crowd who, nice as they were, will always enjoy the sight of the 'expert' caught out by an enthusiastic and well-meaning neophyte (or 'smart alec' as we experts refer to them). And, secondly, I had actually been looking for this whisky but had been unable to find a UK supplier so I wanted to study it carefully rather than neck it there and then (a technical term used in tasting, you'll appreciate).

Us Heit ('Our Father') was founded by distiller Aart van der Linde following an internship in Scotland (note to Scottish distillers – you might have to stop doing this, that's how the Japanese whisky industry got started) and is the original Dutch whisky, dating back to a 3-year-old released in 2005.

They mature their spirit for just 3 years in a variety of casks – information on a side label will gladden the heart of the most obsessive of enthusiasts, detailing the malt type, mashman, date of distillation, stillman, cask type and number, bottling date, strength and so on.

A few comments I found on whisky blogs were very critical of early bottlings, suggesting that the distillery had been pretty casual in their wood selection. If that was so, I can only say that things seem to have improved. The sample I was given, while initially somewhat strange, grew on me and while it's not the best whisky I've ever tried, it was by no means the worst.

Nose Initially boiled cabbage. But then creamy honey and vanilla.

Taste Sweet cereal notes and fruit.

Finish Fades quickly but consistently.

Verdict

35

Producer
Distillery

Visitor Centre
Availability
Price

Millstone
8 Years Old American Oak
Zuidam Distillers BV
Zuidam, Baarle Nassau,
The Netherlands
Yes – tours by appointment
Limited specialists and distillery

www.zuidam.eu

Millstone

8 Years Old American Oak

Zuidam joined Holland's vibrant distilling scene in 1974, when Fred van Zuidam began making genever, gin and vodka. Whisky production began in earnest in 2002, following some earlier, less-than-satisfactory experiments.

Now that they are able to offer fully matured spirit, we can see that the quality stands up happily against some distinguished competition. At 8 years of age, Zuidam offer their Millstone brand, matured alternately in American oak and French oak. The American oak seems to me preferable: there is something strangely reminiscent of good bourbon (I mean this in a good way), while the French oak seems rather one dimensional, though attractive enough.

Not shy of experimentation, they also offer a rye whiskey which struck me as pretty authentically spicy – no doubt other expressions will follow. Demand has been high for Millstone (justifiably so) and supplies are somewhat hard to track down. But production has been increased and new warehousing built, so hopefully availability will improve in the future. It's certainly worth waiting for.

This is still a family-run operation, with a state-of-the-art distillery of 3,600 square metres with 4 brand-new copper stills, over 1,000 oak barrels, 4 production lines and a modern tank storage, all capably managed by the founder's two sons Patrick and Gilbert van Zuidam.

The evidence of enthusiasm for whisky in Holland (at least two dedicated magazines and innumerable clubs) suggests that Millstone has a promising future. With a credible distilling heritage and an impressive track record, this augurs well for Dutch whisky.

Perhaps the Scots should start making genever!

Nose   Fruit and honey; gorse flowers.

Taste   Rich, delightfully spicy and surprisingly complex. Vanilla gives way to cooked pears and soft fruit.

Finish   Consistent and sustained; extended spice notes. Overall pleasant and intriguing.

Verdict ....

....

36

Bushmills Black Bush

Producer	Diageo
Distillery	Old Bushmills, Co. Antrim, Northern Ireland
Visitor Centre	Yes
Availability	Good supermarkets, specialists and distillery
Price	▯

www.bushmills.com

Bushmills
Black Bush

I didn't think I could write enthusiastically about the renaissance of Irish whiskey and only mention whiskies from the Republic. In fairness, most of the running has been made recently by Jameson and Cooley, but that doesn't mean we should ignore the giant Diageo operation in the north.

But then, Bushmills doesn't fit comfortably into a generic 'Irish whiskey' basket, having been somewhat idiosyncratically different during its long history. It didn't, for example, begin triple distilling until the 1930s, but adopted a system closer to that used in Scotland than the one generally employed in other Irish pot stills. Perhaps that's because it's geographically closer to Scotland than Dublin or perhaps it was the influence of Charles Doig, the Scottish architect, who remodelled it in the late 1800s.

Since acquiring Bushmills in June 2005, Diageo have invested heavily in sprucing the old place up, expanding production and rebuilding stocks. There hasn't been a great deal of product innovation yet, at least not compared to their cousins south of the border, but I rather suspect it won't be too long before we hear more from this iconic distillery.[10]

For the moment, they offer a range of single malts and the blended Original and Black Bush but it's probably worth paying a little extra for the Bush; it won the top award for Irish blends at the World Whisky Awards in both 2007 and 2010. It's rich and fruity and would, I suspect, pass as rather more expensive than it actually is in a blind taste test. That's because it contains a healthy proportion of single malt, aged in oloroso sherry casks for around 8 to 10 years before it is introduced to the grain. Which, incidentally, still comes from Midleton, the home of Irish Distillers, former owners of Bushmills.

There is an attractive visitor centre and the strange basalt columns of the Giant's Causeway are only a short drive away.

I view this as something of a sleeping giant, or a brand that's biding its time. Diageo didn't spend all that money buying and expanding it not to have something up their capacious sleeves. Watch this space!

[10] As I proof these pages, they've just announced a honey-flavoured variant.

Nose	Rich and warming. A spiced toffee apple.
Taste	Lots of body; chocolate-coated raisins and nuts. Fruitcake and liquorice.
Finish	Luxurious; sweet and long.

Verdict ....

....

37

Producer
Distillery
Visitor Centre
Availability
Price

Aberfeldy Single Cask Release
John Dewar & Sons Ltd
Aberfeldy, Perthshire, Scotland
Yes
Limited specialists and distillery
☐☐☐☐

www.dewars.com

Aberfeldy
Single Cask Release

The giant Bacardi company bought the Aberfeldy distillery from the even more giant Diageo in March 1998; spent a lot of money on the distillery and got down to the tedious business of laying down stock for future release as a single malt.

The distillery had always been busy so there was no lack of stock, but the vast majority of it was reserved for their blends, which took priority. They improved the blend quality on the standard White Label and introduced some rather nice aged blends at 12 and 18 years (the 18 years in particular is a cracker) and a splendidly packaged luxury blended Scotch known as Signature. With that work all done they turned to the single malt and released a 21-year-old Aberfeldy.

Now things have got even more interesting with a series of single cask releases. The first – a 14-year-old – was issued in the summer of 2011 and sold out quickly through the distillery shop and Royal Mile Whiskies, who had a retail exclusive on it. There were just 185 bottles all at cask strength (a mighty 58.1% abv) and non-chill filtered.

While the success of blended whiskies has ironically kept many more single malt distilleries alive than might otherwise be the case, the price of blending has been the relative anonymity in which many of the distilleries languish today. But it is great news for whisky lovers because this is a seriously under-rated whisky.

The first single cask release went well, so they decided to expand the programme and they now aim to release four different casks annually. You'll have to watch for an announcement and, sadly, break open the piggy bank because it's not cheap. On past form, though, they'll be well worth it.

Slightly fatuously, my tasting note is for the last 14-year-old release, which you're unlikely to find. The current release will be different. But that's all part of the fun.

Nose   Leafy apples, honey and sherry sweetness.

Taste   Lots of weight, but not at the expense of Aberfeldy's delicate heather honey signature.

Finish   Smooth, round and warming.

Verdict ....
....

38

Abhainn Dearg

Producer	Abhainn Dearg
Distillery	Abhainn Dearg, Carnish, Isle of Lewis, Scotland
Visitor Centre	Yes
Availability	Limited specialists and distillery
Price	▢▢▢▢

www.abhainndearg.co.uk

Abhainn Dearg

Let's face it, the island of Lewis (it's in the Outer Hebrides, next stop the USA) is pretty remote by most folks' standards. So when you find out that once you've got to the capital Stornoway, it takes over an hour to drive to Uig and find Abhainn Dearg, you might wonder why anyone would put a distillery there. I certainly did.

My colleague Gavin Smith once went to see it and got stuck on Lewis for three days by a storm. There isn't a lot to do in Stornoway in a gale, take his word for it. I certainly have.

The distillery is the brainchild of Mark Tayburn, a local entrepreneur. As he tells it, he was concerned that the 2011 Royal National Mod, a festival of Scottish Gaelic song, arts and culture, better known to one and all as the 'Whisky Olympics', would be held in Stornoway without there being any locally distilled whisky to drink. Or any *legally distilled* whisky anyway. So he determined to remedy this by building a distillery in time for the thirsty delegates' arrival.

It is, of course, tiny; it has a capacity to produce around 20,000 litres of spirit annually (little Kilchoman alone can do five times that). The curious 'witches hat' stills are apparently modelled on an old illicit still that someone left at the distillery and which is now displayed there for the edification of the curious.

To Mark Tayburn's credit, he aims to produce Lewis whisky from field to bottle and, to this laudable end, has planted ten acres of Golden Promise barley. The use of Golden Promise is something of a throwback, but it worked for The Macallan for many years, so why not…?

This raises two interesting points: there isn't enough barley grown in Scotland to support the whole industry, but smaller producers should certainly be able to source all their supplies from home-grown crops. That being so, could they, in future, claim a sort of superior 'made in Scotland' designation? That would make for an interesting tussle with the big boys!

Nose   Grassy; fruits and mushrooms.

Taste   A little harsh and spirity, but shows promise.

Finish   Fairly abrupt; spice and some citrus hints.

Verdict ....

....

39

Producer
Distillery
Visitor Centre
Availability
Price

Ardbeg Corryvreckan
The Glenmorangie Company Ltd
Ardbeg, Islay, Scotland
Yes
Specialists and distillery
◼◼◼

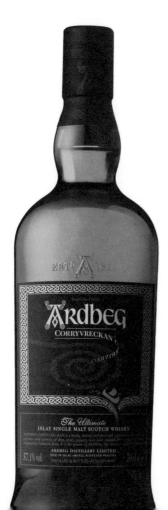

www.ardbeg.com

Ardbeg

Corryvreckan

I've thrown this one in for the peat freaks. In *101 Whiskies* I listed Ardbeg's 10 Years Old and Uigeadail expressions but this takes us to new levels of strength (it's a fearsome 57.1% abv) and taste intensity. So prepare yourself; all too easily you could get sucked into a vortex of turbulent whisky – a veritable whirlpool of flavour, in fact.

That's actually a pretty feeble link to let me explain the name. The Corryvreckan is a whirlpool in the sea off Jura (that's the island next to Islay). There is no shortage of myths and legends surrounding the Corryvreckan but, in full flow when the tides are right, it's an impressive sight, apparently, generating waves of up to 15 feet high (typically, when I went there, it was completely the wrong time of day and it looked like a millpond – perhaps I was looking at the wrong bit?). The author George Orwell, who lived on Jura after World War 2, nearly got himself drowned in it. Maybe he thought his big brother would save him.

Promotional copy for Ardbeg's offering to the water gods makes much punning play on the 'deep and turbulent forces' in this whisky, which is, indeed, a maelstrom of flavour. Originally it was available only as a limited release to members of the Ardbeg Committee but it proved too popular and has now joined the range on a permanent basis.

Because it's so strong, you are going to want to add some water; in which case, you will see this exhibit the classic vortices arising when liquids of different viscosities mix, resulting in the so-called 'viscimetric whorls'. That's true of cask strength whiskies in general but it seemed particularly appropriate to mention it here.

Apart from that, what you need to know about Ardbeg is that it has legions of fans; it markets itself as a feisty outsider when, in fact, it is owned by one of the largest and most successful luxury goods marketing machines in the world (LVMH – ultimate owner of Glenmorangie plc); and it also has a great café in its visitor centre.

Nose   Powerful stuff. Seaweed and tar giving way to dark chocolate and fruits.

Taste   Meaty, morello cherries, plums and plenty of untamed peat. Delightfully complex.

Finish   Intense waves of hot, peppery flavour.

Verdict ....

....

40

Producer
Distillery

Visitor Centre
Availability
Price

Balblair 2001 Vintage
Inver House Distillers Ltd
Balblair, Edderton, Ross-shire,
Scotland
Yes
Specialists and distillery
☐☐

www.balblair.com

Balblair
2001 Vintage

Having spent many years rather over-shadowed by its near neighbour Glenmorangie, Balblair has started to come into its own. A smart new visitor centre (sorry, 'brand home') was opened in 2011 and the string of 'vintage' releases has attracted some interest from canny drinkers.

They make great play of being the only distillery that uniquely releases vintages, though Hammer Head (see number 10) might argue, and why this should make the slightest difference rather escapes me anyway. However, there are some things about the 2001 Balblair expression that set it apart from the earlier releases and we can all cheer now that they are bottling at 46% abv, holding to the whisky's natural colour and no longer chill filtering.

Now that's nothing very special these days, you might say. And you'd be quite correct. But, let's not be churlish; another convert to the path of righteousness, however belated, is always welcome. Arguably, most whisky would be better for a few more degrees of strength and for being bottled without any colouring (that's why they put spirit caramel in there, by the way). As for the risk of a little hazing because it wasn't chill filtered, well, what's a little cloudiness among friends? By the end of the evening, matters are often hazy enough without worrying about slightly murky whisky – the extra creamy mouth feel is more than enough compensation.

Apart from this, when I spoke to the distillery about the 2001 vintage, they were very keen to tell me that the box had been 'slightly reduced in width'. So I promised I'd mention that. Hands up anyone who cares (the Brand Manager is disqualified).

Thought not.

New, slim-line box or no, this is great value. The distillery is delightfully traditional, well worth a visit and deserves to be better known. Think out of the box: try this and give yourself a wee treat.

Nose   Really spicy with loads of lovely vanilla; fresh fruit bursts from the glass. Sweet.

Taste   Distinctive toffee/caramel; more spice notes and half-time orange slices, with just a hint of wood smoke. Panettone.

Finish   The spice dominates the finish, with a mouth-watering rush at the end.

Verdict

....

....

41

Producer The BenRiach Distillery
Company Ltd

Distillery BenRiach, Elgin, Morayshire,
Scotland

Visitor Centre No – you could phone and ask,
though

Availability Specialists

Price

BenRiach
Sherry Matured 12 Years Old

www.benriachdistillery.co.uk

BenRiach
Sherry Matured 12 Years Old

Like a number of the smaller, independently owned distilleries, BenRiach (not a typo, they stick the capital in the middle) releases a bewildering number of expressions and finishes. I counted twenty-seven on the website and that's without the 'Limited Releases', which, in the past, have included Tokaji and Barolo wine finishes, as well as the more normal Sauternes, Port and so on.

It does get rather confusing and hard to follow, unless you're a dyed-in-the-wool enthusiast for this little Speyside distillery. As you probably aren't, it might be best to start with this stunning little dram, which justly collected two big awards at the 2011 International Wine & Spirits Competition. You certainly won't regret it and, because they don't go overboard on lavish packaging, it won't break the bank either.

It's a vatting of whiskies matured in two different styles of sherry cask (oloroso and Pedro Ximenez) and then allowed a marrying period. The result is delightfully rich and satisfying, without overpowering the initial spirit character, as can sometimes be the case with some sherry cask whiskies.

As I have mentioned, the distillery is privately owned, with finance from South African investors. They have also bought Glendronach (which you can visit) and both appear to be prospering. Having been mothballed for so long since it first opened in 1898, it's enormously satisfying to see BenRiach back at work and getting the tender loving care that it deserves.

It's an unusual single malt that will challenge even the hard-core enthusiast to place it accurately. So, not one you'll see every day but worth making its acquaintance. And, if you like this, you can move on through the range, trying the peated Curiositas and Authenticus, as well as the various cask finishes.

Nose   Dried fruits, spices and sherry wood.

Taste   Bread and honey, dried fruits; opens with hints of peat smoke and bursts of banana and barley sugar.

Finish   Long and remarkably smooth.

Verdict

42

Producer	**BIG PEAT**
Distillery	Douglas Laing & Co. Ltd
	A blend from Ardbeg, Bowmore,
	Caol Ila and Port Ellen – all from
	Islay, Scotland
Visitor Centre	No – but you can visit all the
	distilleries they say are in it
Availability	Specialists and some supermarkets
Price	⬜⬜

www.douglaslaingwhisky.com

BIG PEAT

Well, this does exactly what it says on the tin – or flamboyant label to be exact. It's not everyone's cup of tea. Frankly, it's not mine. But if you want peat, then you'll be happy. Very, very happy, because this delivers by the barrow-load. And then some.

This is a blend of malts from Islay – surprise, surprise – designed to dial up the phenol content, the compound found in peat smoke that delivers the smoky, tarry, medicinal (take your pick, you get the idea) taste that 'smoke heads' and 'peat freaks' adore.

Refreshingly, they come clean about what's in the bottle, proudly claiming Ardbeg, Bowmore, Caol Ila and Port Ellen in the 'recipe'. So you know exactly what you're going to get and you can argue long into the night about the exact proportions.

In fairness, it's won a number of awards from groups such as the Malt Maniacs and _Whisky Magazine_, and seems a well-made example of this particular style. It's a good instance of why this book doesn't have scores. I wouldn't score it at all well but someone who likes this style of whisky might then miss out (assuming they paid any attention to what I think).

There's not a lot more to say, really. It's very peaty and it doesn't cost a lot. I won't be buying it, but then that just means there's more out there for the folks who like this kind of thing.

If that's you, you might also like to know that they did a cask strength version for Christmas 2011 which they might just repeat in future years. Now that is extremely peaty. In case you were wondering.

PS There is an _incredibly_ irritating ticking clock sound effect on the relevant web page which I couldn't figure out how to switch off, though it does seem to keep the correct time.

Nose   Guess what? Loads of peat smoke. And other peaty things.

Taste   It's no good asking me. It tastes like a really extreme Islay whisky and that doesn't do it for me. Sorry. If it's your kind of thing, you won't need notes anyway.

Finish   Yup, it's smoky; though it does calm down at the end. Thank goodness.

Verdict ....

....

43

Producer
Distillery
Visitor Centre
Availability
Price

Black Bull 12 Years Old
Duncan Taylor Scotch Whisky Ltd
They won't tell you
No
Specialists
⬜⬜

www.blackbullwhisky.com

Black Bull

12 Years Old

There aren't too many merchant bottlings here but as this company dates back to 1933 we can be reasonably confident they're going to be around for the long haul. Originally based in Glasgow, they now operate out of Huntly in Aberdeenshire and have evolved from the traditional whisky broker (now an endangered species) to become a merchant and bottler with ambitions to open their own distillery – though plans for that appear to have stalled.

Moving from merchant to distiller is a very big step. Some have managed it successfully (Signatory now operate Edradour, and Gordon & MacPhail run Benromach) but it's demanding both financially and managerially. So we'll wish them luck and hope it doesn't distract from the blending business.

Their Black Bull range also dates back to the 1930s and has apparently always had something of a following in the USA. Today the range starts with this 12-year-old expression and carries on through a very limited Special Reserve (grab a bottle if you see it) to a 30- and even a 40-year-old.

The 'entry level' 12-year-old is my pick. It has collected a very respectable number of well-deserved awards and rightly so. This is jolly satisfying, well-made stuff that stands up against some heavyweight competitors, partly because at 50% abv it's a bit of a heavyweight itself.

Honest, unpretentious, amusingly packaged and great value for money, the Black Bull stands out from the shelf and from the crowds. But then, they do sell it under the slogan: 'No bull, just whisky'.

Nose   Meaty, full-flavoured and assertive. Toffee, sherry, vanilla and lemon marmalade toast all clamour for attention. Some smoke hints also.

Taste   A slightly oily nuttiness; fruits and sherry wood. Full bodied, but dilutes well.

Finish   Creamy and satisfying.

Verdict

....

....

44

Bruichladdich The Laddie Ten

Producer	Bruichladdich Distillery Company
Distillery	Bruichladdich, Islay, Scotland
Visitor Centre	Yes
Availability	Specialists, some supermarkets and distillery
Price	⬜⬜

www.bruichladdich.com

Bruichladdich
The Laddie Ten

'We believe that the whisky industry is turning out an increasingly bland, industrial product – for profit, not passion. The domination of global mega-corporations has led to homogeneity, predictability and the worship of the status quo… [we believe] that a spirit should speak of the land and of the people who crafted it.'

Well, amen. But who are these heretics?

It's no surprise, I suppose, to find that they're on Islay. Remote places encourage independent, free-spirited thinking and – whatever else you think about this intransigent, irreverent, irrepressible bunch – they have that in abundance. I'm talking, of course, of Bruichladdich, who celebrated the tenth anniversary of the first distillation under the current ownership in September 2011.

And I embrace The Laddie Ten with open arms because, for the first time, I really understand where this distillery is going. I wasn't alone in finding the plethora of releases and finishes confusing to the point of annoying. And let's not mention the adolescent, chippy attitude that seemed to me to characterise too many of their early public pronouncements. I'm forever reminded of Brando in *The Wild One*: 'What are you against?' the girl asks. 'What have you got?' he fires back.

But now they've matured. Without losing any of their fire, they've developed an intellectually credible position on distilling and are backing it up with excellent products like this. In true Bruichladdich style, it's bottled at 46% abv and the initial release is mostly drawn from bourbon casks, with a few oloroso sherry casks added for body. I think they've set a standard; a reference dram that defines the distillery style and provides a benchmark against which to judge future bottlings.

This is their flagship, therefore, and the place to start a wonderful relationship with this quirky little distillery. The trials and tribulations of independent ownership have been overcome and this whisky vindicates everything they've been saying and doing. The whisky blogosphere loved this. So will you.

Nose   A light, almost delicate nose, with sweet notes and a distinctive bourbon signature; hints of rose water perfume mixed with sea breezes and light citrus.

Taste   Citrus – tangy orange marmalade – spices, nuts, dried fruits and creamy fudge.

Finish   Oak, black pepper, spices and fading citrus.

Verdict ....

....

45

Producer
Distillery

Visitor Centre
Availability
Price

Cutty Sark Storm
The Edrington Group
Another secret – but I'm guessing some of their own is in there (see text)
No
USA, Spain, Greece and UK specialists
⊡⊡

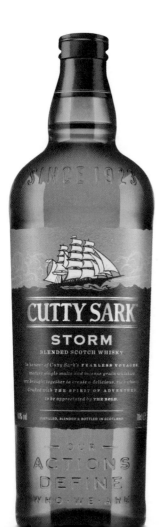

www.cutty-sark.com

Cutty Sark

Storm

I'm very partial to a Cutty Sark and their older blends, especially the 25 Years Old, are superb.

The brand has been in new ownership since April 2010 and there have been quite a few changes, including a new bottle, a tidying up of the range (farewell Cutty Black, which no one really understood anyway) and a greatly increased marketing effort. As part of that, I should mention that they commissioned some of the best drinks writers around to create a Cutty Sark book which I edited (this is the 'declaration of interest' bit). Get one; it's good.

There have been some exciting and different special editions (again, I helped with one that celebrated the connection to Burns' *Tam o' Shanter*) but this Cutty Sark Storm is a permanent addition to the range, and very welcome. It's a premium blended whisky; a little higher in price than the regular bottle, but less than the aged variants and well worth the money.

What they've done is tinker with the blend recipe to increase the percentage of single malts and reduce the amount of grain whisky. At the same time, though, they've used younger grain and slightly older malt whiskies, which has had the effect of increasing the depth of flavour in the mouth feel while retaining the vibrancy contributed by the younger whiskies. All this has been done by a rising star of the blending community, Kirsteen Campbell.

Of course, she has the inestimable advantage of starting with some superb whiskies. The Edrington Group also own Glenrothes, The Macallan and Highland Park, all of which have been long-standing components of Cutty Sark. Just imagine having access to those warehouses!

They call it Storm in reference to Cutty's maritime links. I thought it offered pretty plain sailing in the glass – but it may go down a storm with you.

Nose   Fuller-bodied than the standard Cutty Sark, with more sweetness and marzipan and dough on the nose.

Taste   Rich and creamy; again, more weight and mouth feel than its little sister; nutty and with some smoke in the background.

Finish   Spicy and showing a developing complexity even as it fades.

Verdict ....

....

46

Dewar's
18 Year Old Founder's Reserve

Producer	John Dewar & Sons Ltd
Distillery	This is a blend but it wouldn't surprise me if there was a lot of Aberfeldy in it!
Visitor Centre	Yes – brand home is in Aberfeldy, Perthshire
Availability	Specialists and duty free
Price	■■■

www.dewars.com

Dewar's

18 Year Old Founder's Reserve

I picked out a couple of the Dewar's blends in *101 Whiskies* and felt I had to stop at that. However, having turned over a new leaf, I can bring this one to your attention (you should also check out the Aberfeldy Single Cask Releases – number 37).

Dewar's have always been a company built on blending and, under the influence initially of Tom Aitken and more recently Stephanie MacLeod, they have been going from strength to strength. However, being owned by Bacardi, they tend to ignore the UK market because – in fairness – the UK market tends to ignore luxury blends. Our loss.

The extra aging and the marrying that Dewar's insist on for their more expensive blends, really show to advantage here with great elegance and finesse, but with no loss of power. The heart of the blend, as ever, is the Perthshire single malt Aberfeldy, which lends a lovely heather honey note to the spirit. It's unexpectedly good.

There is one fly in the ointment. This was launched at 43% abv but recent supplies have been coming through at 40% abv. This suggests that it's a victim of its own success as, presumably, stocks have had to be spread a little thinner to cope with demand. The higher strength version picked up a number of awards, including a Best Blend in the World Whiskies Awards in 2007; it will be interesting to see if the latest release can build on that success or if competition judges will mark it down.

Despite this, the Founder's Reserve is a powerful and satisfying dram that offers good value for money. You might find it most easily at the airport, where there seem to be regular offers from Dewar's.

There has to be some benefit to undergoing the ghastly experience of flying.

Nose Sweet, well rounded and full flavoured.

Taste Lots of fruit and honey; sweet but not cloying; a rounded, smoke-free zone.

Finish Steady, consistent and long-lasting. Hints of oak wood at the death.

Verdict

47

Producer
Distillery
Visitor Centre
Availability

Price

Drambuie 15
Drambuie Liqueur Company
No one's saying
No
Specialists, good supermarkets
and duty free
⬜⬜

www.drambuie.com

Drambuie 15

Bear with me. I realise that this isn't actually a whisky but I want you to approach it with an open mind.

Forget the sweet, sticky stuff your mum and dad used to drink after their dinner parties and try to imagine a ready-mixed Rusty Nail in a bottle. That's what we've got here.

Drambuie's glory days came after the war and, up until the mid-1980s, the business was still quietly successful. Then the rot slowly set in: after-dinner liqueurs dropped out of fashion and the company began to lose its way. Some ill-judged acquisitions and a foray into speed boats, fast cars and art collecting didn't help.

A steady decline in sales, compounded by inexperienced management, meant that by 2001 Drambuie was losing over £3 million a year. It seemed that this proudly Scottish business, one of the few remaining in family hands, would inevitably be snapped up by one of the industry's corporate giants.

But radical action was taken. The family relinquished day-to-day control; new, professional management arrived; the art collection, lavish company HQ and several unrelated businesses were sold off; and a new strategy was launched. Slowly things turned round – the bank was repaid, shareholders' funds rebuilt and the company began launching new products in an effort to capture the younger drinker.

Drambuie 15 is probably the whisky drinker's Drambuie: it contains 100% malt whisky, all aged at least 15 years and the significantly reduced sweetness is what leads me to liken it to that Rusty Nail. Try using it in your own cocktails and pretty soon this will become a staple in your drinks cabinet.

It is a fantastic advertisement for what can be done with good Scotch, without bastardising the base ingredient. If only the Scotch whisky establishment would lighten up and allow some product innovation... But sadly the view seems to be that more and tighter regulations are the way to go.

Well, they can't stop me from recommending it. It may not be Scotch but it has whisky in its blood. (See also Compass Box Orangerie – for more heresy.)

Nose   Honey, cloves and aniseed.

Taste   Delightfully spicy, with warm orange notes; honey and vanilla. Smoky hints.

Finish   Smooth, round and warming.

Verdict

48

Producer
Distillery
Visitor Centre
Availability
Price

Glen Deveron 10 Years Old
John Dewar & Sons Ltd
MacDuff, Banff, Scotland
No
Limited specialists
◻◻

No dedicated website

Glen Deveron

10 Years Old

You won't see a lot of this quietly anonymous single malt from the MacDuff distillery. Most of the output is used in the William Lawson and Dewar blends and, so far as single malt goes, owners John Dewar & Sons prefer to concentrate their attention on Aberfeldy.

The distillery is quite modern, dating from 1962, and was state of the art for its time. The Welsh engineer and architect William Delmé-Evans was reputedly involved in the design, but left the project partway through following a disagreement with the then proprietors. Apparently he never spoke of it again. Well, we can credit him here and now, albeit 50 years too late.

It changed hands several times, ending up in Bacardi's ownership. Previously it was owned by Martini & Rossi, who developed substantial volumes for the Lawson's blends in Europe, and that is where Glen Deveron (named after the nearby River Deveron incidentally) is mainly found.

But if you do come across a bottle, most probably of the 10 Years Old official bottling, don't put it back in favour of something more familiar. This probably won't be the most explosive whisky you've ever tried (there is scarcely a hint of smoke) but, if you take the time to explore its subtle complexities, you'll find hidden depths. The MacDuff spirit is held in high regard by the blending industry and that's a reasonable enough recommendation.

There are also some merchant bottlings available, generally at cask strength, and the Malt Maniacs picked out a cask strength bottling for Taiwan in their 2011 Awards. That prompts the thought that, with a little imagination, the distillery bottling could be lifted to 46% abv or higher, which I imagine would greatly enhance it. It's not a lot to ask.

The distillery isn't open to the public and there isn't even a brand website, but perhaps if we all bought the odd bottle the proprietors might overcome their curious reticence.

Nose   Floral and grassy. Light but not lacking in charm.

Taste   Bran flakes, vanilla and freshly cut melon.

Finish A little pepper snap and the smoke comes in unexpectedly at the end.

Verdict

49

Producer
Distillery

Visitor Centre
Availability
Price

Glenfarclas 40 Years Old
J & G Grant
Glenfarclas, Ballindalloch,
Banffshire, Scotland
Yes
Specialists and distillery
□□□□■

www.glenfarclas.co.uk

Glenfarclas

40 Years Old

Expect to pay around £300 for this. But be happy: you've snagged one of *the* great bargains in the world of whisky.

Despite what their rivals charge for a bottle of this age and quality (and you could easily pay well into four figures), Glenfarclas aim to sell whisky that people can buy to enjoy, not collect or – worse still – 'invest'.

Of course, if you want a ritzy box, fancy crystal decanter, handsome book, medallions, a 'certificate of authenticity' and need tasting notes by a self-styled 'superstar' whisky writer, you'll need to look elsewhere. Glenfarclas eschew these props in favour of their standard bottle and a simple tube. It's whisky for drinking, not looking at. If you need the reinforcement of elaborate packaging and a third party endorsement, this probably isn't for you.

On the other hand, if you know your own mind; you like classic, sherry-matured Speyside whisky, and consider one of the few family-owned independent pure whisky distillers left in business worthy of your support then you're going to love this.

Apart from the stripped-down packaging, the other reason they can sell whisky at this price is twofold: it is a family concern and, at the end of the 1960s, they made a decision never to be wholly reliant on blending contracts. So they started laying down stocks for their own use and, because they are able to ignore the City totally, they could leave it to mature for future generations. Consequently, they were able to produce and store significant quantities using the very best old sherry casks that money could buy. Now that whisky is ready: aren't we the lucky ones?

Incidentally, they do very occasionally hire whisky writers: I had the privilege last year of writing the commemorative book that marked the distillery's 175th year of licensed operation. With the money you save on this bottle, do us both a favour and buy a copy.

Nose   Benchmark sherried Speyside, with masses of dark fruits, then coffee and chocolate.

Taste   Hints of a Terry's dark chocolate orange. Massive mouth feel and loads of dried fruits, prunes and a sinuous oak note.

Finish   Just goes on for ever, fading with dignity and restraint. Unlike most whisky writers!

Verdict

50

Producer
Distillery

Visitor Centre
Availability

Price

Glenfiddich
15 Year Old Solera Reserve

William Grant & Sons Distillers Ltd
Glenfiddich, Dufftown, Banffshire,
Scotland

Yes

Specialists, supermarkets, duty
free and distillery
⬜⬜

www.glenfiddich.co.uk

Glenfiddich
15 Year Old Solera Reserve

As I've said before, all whisky lovers owe William Grant & Sons a vote of thanks for being the one company that took single malt whisky seriously at a time when the whole of the rest of the industry was focusing on blends. Some other small independents took up the fight, but Grants were the pioneers and deserve the kudos for that.

Not that their blends are anything shabby, it should be said (see number 54), but they do really stand out for their long-term commitment to their single malts – Glenfiddich and The Balvenie.

What we have here is a 15-year-old Glenfiddich that, uniquely, has been matured in three types of oak cask (sherry, bourbon and new oak), before being married in a 'solera' style Oregon pine vat. Year on year, this solera vat is never emptied but is always kept at least half full. The result is a deliciously harmonious and intense whisky which gets more complex and intriguing every year. I've stood on top of a ladder and breathed in the heady aromas straight from the vat. It was all I could do not to jump in. You could get delightfully light-headed simply nosing it in the warehouse. If you could capture the aroma, you could sell it as room spray.

This is lovely, rich, intense whisky and is actually a little bit of a bargain. It might even surprise a few malt snobs, who are inclined to dismiss Glenfiddich because it is fairly ubiquitous – but that's the price of success.

But here's what they should do to make it that little bit better: bottle it at cask strength or at least up the strength to 46% abv. Having had the privilege of trying it straight from the vat before it was reduced for bottling, I'm here to tell you that this one simple change would transform an excellent whisky into a transcendentally great one.

Perhaps, just perhaps, one day they will.

Nose   Intense honey and sherry sweetness.

Taste   Lots of weight; lush and fruity, with a bourbon-like sweetness and intensity. Baked apple, cinnamon, oak, fudge and the signature Glenfiddich pears.

Finish   Smooth, round and warming.

Verdict ....

....

51

Producer
Distillery

Visitor Centre
Availability
Price

Glenglassaugh Revival
Glenglassaugh Distillery Co. Ltd
Glenglassaugh, Portsoy,
Aberdeenshire, Scotland
Yes
Limited specialists and distillery
◻◻

www.glenglassaugh.com

Glenglassaugh

Revival

I was fortunate enough to have the great pleasure to be in the still house at Glenglassaugh when the first new make from this little distillery – mothballed since 1986 but recently reopened – ran on 16 December 2008. Even more fortunately, the new spirit was clean, grassy and aromatic, holding out great promise for the matured whisky.

Legally it became Scotch whisky precisely three years later. Now, this presents a problem for the distillery: do they bottle and sell it immediately for some much-needed ready cash or do they hold on and continue to mature it? If they sell it now there will definitely be a demand, but every drop they sell today means less will be available for the future when the whisky may taste better and will likely command a higher price. It's a conundrum.

Until very recently you wouldn't have seen a 3-year-old single malt whisky but there has been a trend (or perhaps, more accurately, a fashion) to release some younger whisky to satisfy the curiosity of enthusiasts who want to understand the maturation process. Glenglassaugh has built a small following, especially in Europe, and with them in mind they decided to bottle at least some of the initial production.

Up until now it's been known as much for its unlikely renaissance as for its medal-winning old whisky, so there was great curiosity about this dram.

In an interesting experiment, the very first cask, a refill butt that was filled on that first cask filling day in 2008, was emptied and refilled into two smaller casks on 16 December 2010. These smaller casks were a first-fill ex-Pedro Ximenez sherry hogshead and a first-fill ex-Palo Cortado sherry hogshead. On 16 September 2011 the whiskies were returned from these two casks into the original butt and married for a period of exactly three months before being bottled. Radical stuff.

Having excited you about that, the bad news is that they all immediately sold out. But you can now get Glenglassaugh Revival and, by buying it, you'll be supporting a renovated, independent distillery that came back from the grave. It's an inspiring tale (not to blow my own trumpet again but I also wrote a book about this, but that's another story).

No tasting notes because it is evolving rapidly and the bottle you get will be different from the one I tasted. Bet you it's good, though.

Verdict ....

52

Producer
Distillery

Visitor Centre
Availability
Price

Glengoyne The Teapot Dram
Ian MacLeod Distillers Ltd
Glengoyne, Dumgoyne, near
Killearn, Glasgow, Scotland
Yes
Distillery only
■■■

www.glengoyne.com

Glengoyne
The Teapot Dram

You can buy this online, but it's much more fun to go to the distillery (it's just outside Glasgow) and pick up a bottle yourself while taking one of the excellent tours. Quite a few distilleries offer exclusive distillery-only bottles these days (they love the fact they take all the profit that otherwise goes to a distributor and retailer) but I've restricted myself to just this one. That's because the distillery is in one of Scotland's more accessible locations and because it was the first distillery I ever visited, on my honeymoon, so I have a soft spot for it.

You couldn't get The Teapot then. But, if I had known, I could have asked for a dram from the teapot. The story goes that up until the early 1980s, Glengoyne's men were given three large drams of cask strength whisky every day – breakfast, lunch and afternoon break.

Once a week the Brewer, Ron Low, and the excise men would select the best first-fill sherry cask they could find to become that week's dram. However, if the younger men didn't want one of their drams, they would pour it into the old copper teapot that sat in the rest room. The more seasoned drinkers would then help themselves to additional drams from the teapot throughout the day – everyone was happy. Until health and safety legislation put paid to such a debauched, degrading and sordid practice, of course.

Oops, sorry about that.

'Dramming' was actually common practice across Scotland. The Teapot Dram is a pleasant, if somewhat sanitised, echo of those days and we don't have to turn damp barley, shovel out mash tuns and manhandle heavy casks before drinking a drop.

Ah, the good old days.

NB: Health and Safety alert – this comes at around 59% abv, so take some water with it.

Nose   It is first-fill sherry, so loads of brown sugar, dried fruits and spice.

Taste   Explodes in the mouth; rich and very lively. Fruit and nut chocolate, with stewed fruits, liquorice root and oak wood.

Finish   Fades slowly.

Verdict ....

....

53

Producer
Distillery

Visitor Centre
Availability
Price

Glenmorangie Finealta
The Glenmorangie Company Ltd
Glenmorangie, Tain, Ross-shire,
Scotland
Yes
Widespread

www.glenmorangie.com

Glenmorangie

Finealta

We can't really miss out Glenmorangie, a long-standing favourite among whisky fans and, in its independent days, one of the early stalwarts of the single malt market. But, from its rather confusing range, which one?

Not, I think, the Nectar d'Or which seems to me over-influenced by the use of Sauternes casks. Nor the immodestly named Pride – with its elaborate packaging accounting for too much of the £2,500 price tag. And we all know about Original, so there's no point going on about that. But that's three name checks. Time to choose.

And the winner is… Finealta. Somehow it feels rather contrived to have to discover that 'Finealta' means 'elegant' in Gaelic; and I cannot explain why it has a Gaelic name when it comes in a Cognac-like bottle, but such are the mysteries of marketing. Many and varied are the changes that have been introduced since Glenmorangie was sold in October 2004 to the French luxury brand giants LVMH.

Still, when you've cut through all that, you find a *very interesting* whisky. Glenmorangie is noted for its delicate style (don't say 'light', that's not fair – you have to concentrate and it will reward you) but here it has been mildly peated and matured partly in sherry casks. That would seem almost heretical for Glenmorangie but apparently it has historical antecedents. According to a distiller's notebook from 1903, malt was dried using peat – not so sure about sherry casks back then but let's not get picky, because…

…the result is really quite delightful. To have achieved a fresh take on a whisky that is rooted in distilling lore and tradition is more than impressive. There is no need to get bogged down in the back story, this is a whisky to savour and enjoy.

I think it's one of the best new/old things I've seen in a long time.

Nose   Initially, a beguiling perfumed sweetness that gives way to the signature lime and orange zest.

Taste   The smoke arrives gently on the palate, then fresh fruits, marmalade and mild curry spices all mingle through.

Finish   Holds nicely together, with the spice notes adding complexity and intrigue.

Verdict

54

Grant's 25 Year Old

Producer	William Grant & Sons Distillers Ltd
Distillery	Twenty-five of them, as it's 25 years old
Visitor Centre	Yes – brand home is at Glenfiddich
Availability	Limited specialists and duty free
Price	▢▢▢▢

www.grantswhisky.com

Grant's

25 Year Old

Premium blends don't really get the attention they deserve in the home of Scotch whisky, so it's great to be able to bring to your notice one or two very special whiskies that you might otherwise ignore.

Grant's 25 Year Old blend is one such. It was only created in 2009, was trialled in duty free shops during 2010 and 2011, and is only now being released to domestic markets, for the very good reason that there isn't very much of it.

The blend uses twenty-five different whiskies, including grain from Grant's own Girvan distillery (the story of which is rather remarkable) and rare single malts from distilleries no longer in existence. Each individually numbered batch has been married for several months for depth and complexity, producing an exceptional whisky full of warmth and character.

Inevitably these luxurious old whiskies are expensive. But, by and large, you do get what you pay for, and the best blends represent the zenith of whisky craftsmanship with a multi-dimensional character rarely seen elsewhere. By the standards of these things, it's not over-packaged either so you're not paying (much) for a fancy box.

As an independent firm of long standing, Grants have access to wonderful stocks of their own whiskies, most notably Glenfiddich and The Balvenie. In their mature expressions these are quite superb. When you combine that base of quality with their experience, know-how and single-minded commitment to whisky blending, the results can only be admired.

And, as a footnote, it's worth remembering that, although the firm may be better known for single malt, their range of blended whiskies sold nearly 5 million cases in 2010 – a value of over $1 billion at the retail level. That's a lot of whisky. And this 25 Year Old is at the very top of that pyramid, so give it some respect, please!

Nose   Orange sponge cake and custard. Mouth-watering and very appealing.

Taste   Citrus; fruit cake; dark fruits – plums and prunes; then coffee and dark chocolate. Sweet sherry cask maturation at its best. Takes water well.

Finish   Very extended, smooth, rounded and consistent.

Verdict ....

....

55

Great King Street
Artist's Blend

Producer	Compass Box Whisky Company
Distillery	Men on a mission
Visitor Centre	No
Availability	Mainly UK, USA and France
Price	⬜⬜

www.compassboxwhisky.com

Great King Street
Artist's Blend

If you read the last book, you'll know that I really do love almost everything that Compass Box Whisky Company do, so I hope that my friends there will forgive me when I suggest there's a slightly messianic quality to their work.

Take the new blended Scotch that they launched in the summer of 2011, Great King Street – Artist's Blend. If the name wasn't pretentious enough, here's what company founder John Glaser had to say about it in the original press release:

'This is more than a brand; it's a mission. A mission to get people – all people – to take a fresh look at Blended Scotch; to join in the Rebirth of the Blend: in how Blends are made, how they are viewed, how they are consumed.'

Gosh! The 'Rebirth of the Blend' no less. Well, that's ambitious – but I was hardly aware that blended Scotch needed rebirthing (with over 92% of the world market for Scotch whisky, it's hardly missing in action). It sounds rather unpleasant actually, with echoes of hippy, cod-psychology or the demented ramblings of an extreme religious cult.

So it took me a day or two to get past the hype and open the sample they sent me.

But I've got to be fair: this is good, really good. In fact, it's great. Smooth, warm and elegant, with oak, vanilla and spice all over the mouth – so forgive and forget the over-the-top embellishments on the copy and website – just get some. Quick!

In fact, do get some quick, because the challenge for Compass Box is that their own success may – just may – contain the seeds of their downfall. For it's one thing to produce fabulous whisky on a hand-crafted scale but, if they get the success they deserve, they're going to have to produce lots and lots more of it, and that's when things will get really tough.

Nose	Rich and warming; sweet with citrus hints and ripe fruits (peach and mango).
Taste	Liquorice; sweet and appealing; mouth coating with wood notes; light fruit cake and peaches and cream.
Finish	Smooth, round and consistently appealing. The liquorice note lingers nicely.

Verdict ....

....

56

Highland Park – All of them!

Producer	Highland Distillers
Distillery	Highland Park, Kirkwall, Orkney, Scotland
Visitor Centre	Yes
Availability	Widespread
Price	From under £20 to £10,000

www.highlandpark.co.uk

Highland Park
All of them!

I went slightly overboard in the first *101 Whiskies* and nominated four whiskies from Highland Park. Having decided that I would try to avoid giving more than one mention to any one brand, I was left with a problem. So I'm simply going to cheat and nominate all of them (my book, my rules!).

From which you can reasonably deduce that this is probably my single favourite whisky of all time. If you were buying, I'd probably have one of these. But it's not just about the whisky: to understand Highland Park you really have to try to appreciate Orkney, which means going there and spending some time absorbing its unique history, landscape and atmosphere. If any whisky can be said to exemplify the spirit of a place then this must be a contender.

The distillery can be traced back to 1798 and, even before single malts became fashionable, its whisky was renowned for its quality as a 'self' whisky. In 1883 it was served to the King of Denmark and the Emperor of Russia and the party pronounced it 'the finest they had ever tasted'. Whether or not they knew anything about whisky I have no idea, but in 1930 Aeneas MacDonald (who did) described Highland Park as 'one of the small first class, the *premiers crus*, as it were, of Scotch whiskies.' Try, incidentally, to get hold of a copy of MacDonald's little book *Whisky* – the first modern whisky book and, to this day, one of the most lyrical.

In recent years, Highland Park has gathered a global reputation and the distillery have responded by releasing a wide range of whiskies. The 'core expressions' range from 12 to 40 years old and there are various limited bottlings that commemorate events and personalities as varied as Orkney Rugby Club, Earl Magnus and Leif Eriksson. Many are enthusiastically collected, although I hope they won't overdo the 'collectable' releases. They seem to have come thick and fast lately and, fun though they are, it can quickly feel exploitative.

At the top of the pyramid is a venerable 50 Year Old. By the standards of these ultra-premium releases, it's relatively modestly priced at £10,000 and rather tastefully packaged.

Just to whet your appetite I've illustrated it opposite. Like I say – my book, my rules!

No tasting notes. I promise that I don't work for the distillery but I can guarantee that almost any bottle you buy will represent an exceptional mix of quality and value. (Ten thousand quid might be pushing it, though.)

Verdict

57

Producer
Distillery
Visitor Centre

Availability
Price

**Johnnie Walker
Double Black**
Diageo
Classified Top Secret
Brand home is Cardhu Distillery,
Speyside, Scotland
Widespread
▢▢

www.johnniewalker.com

Johnnie Walker
Double Black

It's now something of a cliché in whisky circles to pay lip service to blends. Which is, I suppose, something of an improvement on the recent past when they were looked down upon as the poor relation of single malt. But it can hardly be said too often that Scotland would not have the amazing number of distilleries it does, were it not for the success of blends. And they also still account for the vast majority of Scotch whisky sold in the world.

All of this can be traced back to the innovative and entrepreneurial 'whisky barons' of the nineteenth century – men like James Buchanan, John and Tommy Dewar, and Alexander Walker. Alexander Walker's family firm was established in Kilmarnock in 1820 but really got into its stride in 1887 when he launched his Old Highland Whisky, eventually developing the Extra Special variant around 1906. This is the bloodline for Black Label (1909) and this, the latest expression, Double Black (2011).

Today the firm is owned by Diageo and their resources mean they can devote the necessary research effort to replicating the original recipes (Alexander's blending notebook still survives and is regularly referred to) and maintaining the integrity of the house style. It also helps that they have more distilleries than anyone else. Sometimes big is good.

Standard Black Label is greatly admired within the whisky industry for its earthy, smoky character, offset by rich fruit notes, creamy vanilla aromas and a certain freshness and vivacity. With Double Black they have increased the 'island smoky' character, while using more heavily charred casks that help showcase the character of the blend components.

As readers will have noted, I am not a huge fan of assertive, heavily peated whiskies, finding them in general too one-dimensional (you may love them; that's fine). This is different – smoky, yes, but balanced and well integrated.

The very ubiquity of the Walker blends might lead you to overlook them. That would be a mistake. Their style is distinctive, powerful and consistent. It is also a kind of historical document that connects us through the meticulous scholarship of the Diageo blenders and archivists to an important period in whisky's history.

Nose   Peat and heather. Surprisingly subtle and inviting.

Taste   Refreshing, lively and well balanced. Smooth and sophisticated smoke that beguiles as it dancies on the palate.

Finish   Long and consistent.

Verdict ....

....

58

Producer
Distillery
Visitor Centre
Availability
Price

Kilchoman 100% Islay
Kilchoman Distillery Co. Ltd
Kilchoman, Islay, Scotland
Yes
Specialists and distillery

www.kilchomandistillery.com

Kilchoman

100% Islay

The bad news is that this is in limited supply and, frankly, expensive for such young whisky.

But allow me to explain why you should buy it anyway.

The sun doesn't always shine on Islay. In fact, sometimes it feels you could be blown off the island by some lusty gales – when you're not in danger of being washed off by the torrents of rain.

For one day only, though, the weather was on its best behaviour: for the launch of Kilchoman's 100% Islay release. As you know if you read *101 Whiskies*, Kilchoman is a farm distillery established as recently as 2005 and was the first to be built on Islay for 124 years. However, what you might not know is that it's been something of a struggle for founder Anthony Wills (and his long-suffering family), so he could be forgiven a few tears and a slight choke in his voice when he proudly announced the release of the first true 100% Islay whisky – produced entirely from barley grown, malted, distilled, matured and bottled at the distillery.

He said: *'I set this project up because I wanted to do things slightly differently, and show the world we could produce a single malt where all the ingredients were produced locally.'* He went on to describe raising the funds and setting up the distillery as a *'monumental journey'*. He wasn't kidding.

While local pipers serenaded its arrival, we had the opportunity to taste this 50% abv dram, which has spent a little over 3 years in a combination of refill and fresh bourbon barrels. The importance of the fact that it is 100% Islay in its provenance can't be over-stated.

The launch was a huge, culturally significant moment and the best of what whisky stands for: among friends and colleagues, in the open air, toasting a little piece of history with some very fine whisky.

And if you buy a bottle you can join in.

Nose Peat, citrus, lemon zest and pear drops.

Taste A delightfully teasing, light, oily mouth feel and a granity, mineralic character with lemon cheesecake.

Finish More soft peat; mixed fruits. Very lively.

Verdict ....

....

59

Producer
Distillery
Visitor Centre
Availability
Price

Longmorn 16 Year Old
Chivas Brothers Ltd
Longmorn, Speyside, Scotland
No
Specialists
■■■

www.chivasbrothers.com

Longmorn
16 Year Old

Longmorn has long been in demand by the blending industry, valued as a 'top dressing', and in 1924 was considered to be a 'crack Highland malt' – high praise indeed. That in part explains its relative anonymity: its owners, Chivas Brothers, need most of the distillery's output for their Chivas Regal and Ballantine's blends, and what they don't want they can swap within the industry for the other whiskies that they do require.

In fact, there is only this one official bottling and, a few years ago, it was the controversial replacement for a much-loved 15-year-old expression. The latter was very slightly lower in strength (45% versus 48% abv) and came in rather more modest packaging – and at a somewhat lower price.

Its fans (and there were a good few) were not overly impressed when this 16-year-old version was launched and their preferred tipple was withdrawn. At the time I had some sympathy for that view; though I was very glad to see greater emphasis being placed on the whisky.

I've rather come round to this version, however. Longmorn deserves to be better known and this is a great example of what a Speyside whisky should taste like.

The distillery was founded in 1893 by John Duff, who earlier had helped to establish Glenlossie. I feel a great personal attachment to Duff: his family ran a number of small farmhouse distilleries in Perthshire during the early part of the nineteenth century, eventually closing them around 1876 in favour of a move to Speyside. I now live on the site of one of Duff's abandoned distilleries, which later saw service as a dairy and hen house.

Poor Duff! He lost most of his money in the Pattison's crash and by 1909 was forced into bankruptcy. If only he could have held on to his shares in Longmorn, he might have pulled through.

Sadly, in keeping with its low profile, there is no visitor centre. However, the distillery is sometimes opened during the Speyside Whisky Festival.

Nose   Floral and fruity, with coconut (gorse flowers) and the elusive 'pineapple' note so desired in Speyside malts.

Taste   Full-bodied, nutty and spicy, with a minty note.

Finish   Again nutty and quite drying.

Verdict ....

....

**60**

Producer
Distillery

Visitor Centre
Availability
Price

Orangerie Whisky Infusion
Compass Box Whisky Company
Probably Cameron Bridge grain
and a Highland malt from Diageo
No
Mainly UK, USA and France
⬛⬛

www.compassboxwhisky.com

Orangerie
Whisky Infusion

OK, I apologise. After being criticised for including four entries from Highland Park in the last book I swore there would be no multiple entries here. And, just to further confound you (and give the barrack room lawyers plenty to niggle about) this isn't strictly speaking a whisky at all.

But it cries out to be tried. Orangerie is a 'whisky infusion' – a term invented by the proprietors to describe what the rest of us would call a liqueur, except that it's not sweet so it isn't really a liqueur either. You'll have guessed by now that it comes from the Compass Box team, who seem to delight in confounding the rules of the Scotch whisky establishment, while making really great products.

However, getting lost in nomenclature isn't really the point. What we have here is a really rather good blended whisky that is infused with the hand-zested peel of Navalino oranges, Indonesian cassia bark and Sri Lankan cloves. At one point, company founder John Glaser peeled the oranges himself in his own kitchen and supplies of this nectar were very strictly limited. In the past, Orangerie was only bottled once a year, only a few people really knew about it and I suspect they tried to keep the secret to themselves! I liked to surprise people with it, but only if I really liked them. It is that good.

However, production has been expanded somewhat and you'll be able to track down a bottle, now in the full 70cl size (I still prefer the old packaging). You can drink it neat, chill it over lots of ice, or even experiment with your own cocktail ideas – it encourages that kind of free thinking.

You will find orange notes in some whiskies. Here you'll find some whisky notes among the oranges.

Nose   Plenty of oranges, obviously. Then the spice notes hit and, well, it's time to start drinking.

Taste   The first shock is how dry it is; then bitter oranges, followed by spice rolling all over your tongue, which is, by now, in a perverted sort of ecstasy.

Finish   Curiously warming and sustained.

Verdict ....

....

61

Producer	
Distillery	
Visitor Centre	
Availability	
Price	

**Port Askaig Harbour
19 Years Old**

The Whisky Exchange
Undisclosed, Islay, Scotland
Retail outlet at Vinopolis, London
Vinopolis and online
▢▢▢

www.thewhiskyexchange.com

Port Askaig Harbour
19 Years Old

I wasn't going to include any so-called 'merchant releases' here because they can be a little patchy and the distilleries concerned tend to look down on them. Third party bottlers also come and go, and because their access to stock is limited, it's hard to be sure that a consistent quality is maintained.

However, as I know so many people love Islay's peated whiskies and as the group behind this is rather more substantial, I have made an exception.

Port Askaig is the main terminal for the ferry to Islay. There is a decent pub there, a small shop, a large car park for the ferry and, just up the coast, Diageo's giant Caol Ila distillery. Now, you can buy official releases of Caol Ila with the name on the bottle but might 'Port Askaig' be a hint to the whisky's origins? I'll leave it up to you to puzzle that one out. I'm saying nothing.

The bottler behind this is The Whisky Exchange who have a splendid shop at the Vinopolis wine exhibition by London's Borough Market (with some wonderfully enthusiastic and knowledgeable staff) and they also run an excellent mail order service. It's a substantial and well-established business with a high reputation to maintain.

So, in selecting the casks for this little puppy you can be sure that they know what they're doing. Their aim is to offer a mellow, approachable Islay style; something a bit different from the heavy-duty, south coast malts; something that looks and tastes like medium-peated traditional Islay whisky, plain and simple. Hence the retro feel to the packaging and the decision to bottle at around 46% abv without colouring or chill filtration.

All the Port Askaigs so far have been from bourbon or refill bourbon casks, and they allow the batches a decent marriage time before bottling. If you like this style, it's well-balanced, natural, approachable whisky that calls for a second glass.

Nose   Sweet and floral; orange blossom, soap and faint chlorine.

Taste   Dry powdery paper. Lots of peat smoke develops in the mouth.

Finish   Peppery with lemon notes.

Verdict ....

....

62

**Royal Lochnagar
Selected Reserve**

Producer	Diageo
Distillery	Royal Lochnagar, Ballater, Aberdeenshire, Scotland
Visitor Centre	Yes
Availability	Specialists, some supermarkets and distillery
Price	

www.malts.com

Royal Lochnagar
Selected Reserve

This extremely charming little distillery is the smallest in the mighty Diageo empire and, if you only ever visited one distillery in your life, this could be it. For the rubber-necking tourist in us all, it is conveniently close to Balmoral Castle and estate, Scottish holiday home to the British royal family. You can tell if they're at home because there will be a few bored-looking paparazzi hanging around hoping to catch them doing something stupid. As if!

The royal connection goes back to 1848. Queen Victoria and her husband Prince Albert had just acquired the Balmoral estate and they sent a footman round to borrow a cup of sugar. He returned to the castle very drunk, for which crime he was transported to Tasmania where he founded the Australian distilling industry. Much of Lochnagar's 1848 production was consumed as 'evidence' at his trial.

Actually, I made that up. In fact, the socially adept distillery owner John Begg, knowing of the Prince's desire 'to make himself acquainted with all things mechanical' invited his neighbours for a 'wee refreshment' and was rewarded the very next day with a visit from the Queen, Prince Albert and their three eldest children, who toured the distillery and sampled the whisky. The astute Mr Begg received a Royal Warrant as a result, no doubt to the considerable chagrin of his envious rivals. However, Victoria was no connoisseur, as apparently she would mix the whisky with her claret – a combination that has strangely failed to catch on either here or in France.

Hence the 'Royal' moniker, shared only with Royal Brackla (which Diageo also used to own, but sold to Bacardi). Anyway, like a lot of distillery marketing, it doesn't really have a great deal of relevance to the present day, so let's move on.

The main point is the intimate scale of the distillery, which is scrupulously maintained as a showpiece. Unusually, most production is reserved for sale as single malt; the balance goes into Diageo's luxury blends, such as Johnnie Walker Blue Label, which is all the assurance you need.

Nose   Toffee, malt, vanilla and honey.

Taste   More caramel notes, oranges, liquorice and nuts.

Finish   Gentle and warming, with delicate floral hints.

Verdict ....

....

63

Producer
Distillery
Visitor Centre
Availability
Price

Royal Salute 21 Year Old
Chivas Brothers Ltd
A mystery
No
Specialists and duty free
■■■■

www.royalsalute.com

Royal Salute

21 Year Old

Believe it or not, you can pay up to $200,000 (plus local taxes) for a bottle of the ultimate Royal Salute blend, their Tribute to Honour. Mind you, the blender will come round to your house to deliver it and it does have 413 individual diamonds on the bottle and a label made of silver and gold.

Sounds rather vulgar, if you ask me. (I'm just sulking because they wouldn't let me taste it. Can't imagine why not.)

For a rather more reasonable £100 or so you can have the 'entry level' Royal Salute blend at 21 years old in your choice of a red, green or blue ceramic decanter (or, as they would prefer you to say, ruby, emerald or sapphire). The blue (sorry, sapphire) is the biggest seller. I'm personally rather partial to the green one, but the whisky all tastes the same. Which is very good.

Luxury blends like this don't really feature in the UK, or even very much in Europe, where single malts tend to dominate the higher-priced end of the market, but they are huge in the emerging BRIC countries (Brazil, Russia, India and China), where distillers such as Chivas Brothers are investing enormous sums of money.

This kind of product is associated with prestige, achievement and royalty (the original blend was created in 1953 following Queen Elizabeth II's coronation, all of which plays very well into the hands of an aspirational buyer looking for the reassurance of status and ostentatious luxury. Even if there are no diamonds on this bottle.

But it ill behoves the whisky snob to ignore whiskies like this, or to forget that on their success is predicated the continued existence of his or her favourite single malt. Lots of lovely good things go into blends like this and if you deny their existence you deny yourself a real treat.

If you want to splash out, there is the more expensive 38 Year Old Stone of Destiny and, above that, the 62 Gun Salute. If you can run to the Tribute to Honour, though, please give me a call.

Nose   Some subtle smoke, fruit (pears and kumquats) and pepper.

Taste   Very rounded and exceptionally smooth; fruit juice, vanilla and chocolate.

Finish   Stable and consistent; very elegant and satisfying.

Verdict ....

....

64

Producer
Distillery
Visitor Centre
Availability
Price

Sheep Dip Old Hebridean
Spencerfield Spirit Co. Ltd
See the text where all is revealed
No
Limited specialists
▢▢▢

www.spencerfieldspirit.com

Sheep Dip
Old Hebridean

I mentioned Spencerfield's Sheep Dip in *101 Whiskies*. If you liked that, you'll love this limited release. Although, by now, stocks may be running low and you'd be well advised to get moving if you want some. Which you do.

But just to reprise, Spencerfield Spirits is not the usual Scotch whisky company. For one thing, they are based on a farm with a historic link to the USA: James Anderson, George Washington's distiller, worked here before setting sail for his new career at Mount Vernon.

For another, unlike most small drinks companies, you'll find their unusually named brands (Sheep Dip and Pig's Nose) in über-trendy bars around the world as well as in well-established style icons like the Waldorf Astoria.

And, for a third thing, CEO Alex Nicol is far from the usual Scotch whisky chief: certainly he's the only one whose desk is located in a former livery stable. When I went to talk about Old Hebridean, I found him bouncing around with excitement at several new product ideas ('Try this!' he'd exclaim at intervals). After that, we went to meet his pigs. And then we ate them, one sausage at a time.

From a standing start Alex and his wife Jane have built Spencerfield to a seven-figure turnover with a mixture of good products, innovative marketing and a lot of solid hard work. (For years they drove around country fairs selling out of the back of a van – 'One bottle at a time,' recalls Alex.)

Right, that's enough of a panegyric.

Old Hebridean 1990 is a blend of aged island and Highland single malt whiskies. Apparently it contains 19-year-old Dalmore, 21-year-old Fettercairn and 25-year-old Ardbeg, which were vatted together when young and then aged for 15 more years. I have no idea at all why it would occur to anyone to do this but the result is a revelation. I only wish they'd bottled it at 46% abv.

My spies tell me there's still some left. Get it while you can.

Nose   Sherry, ripe plums, stewed prunes and some peat.

Taste   Loads more peat smoke, battling with some meaty notes, old-fashioned toffees and a light citrus element.

Finish   Plenty of that smoke, but tempered by richer notes (Dalmore?) and years of maturation.

Verdict ....

....

65

Producer
Distillery

Visitor Centre
Availability
Price

**The Dalmore
King Alexander III**
Whyte & Mackay Ltd
Dalmore, Alness, Ross-shire,
Scotland
Yes
Specialists and distillery

www.thedalmore.com

The Dalmore

King Alexander III

The Dalmore continues to release a stream of very high-priced whiskies which they describe as 'investments'. I would list them but they really don't need any more publicity. As you will have read in the Introduction I am not a fan of investing in whisky: in fact, I think it's a very poor idea indeed. Please don't do it.

However, you might want to 'invest' in a bottle of this, which you should duly drink. Lest we forget that is why they make whisky.

The handsome red deer antlers on the bottle are The Dalmore's logo. This bottle commemorates the quick thinking of a certain Mackenzie who, in 1263, saved King Alexander who was being attacked by a stag (they're vicious beasts when provoked; several people are killed each year by enraged stags[11]). Later, the Mackenzie family owned the distillery so adopted the antlers to acknowledge their celebrated ancestor.

All pretty tenuous, but it makes for a pretty story and an attractive bottle so let's not hear any complaints. What about the whisky, I hear you cry?

Well, it's a single malt, but with a difference. To make this King Alexander III, Whyte & Mackay's Master Distiller Richard Paterson has selected a number of differently aged French wine casks, Madeira drums, sherry butts, Marsala barrels, Port pipes and bourbon barrels from Kentucky. A remarkable feat of blending that, unusually, doesn't carry an age declaration. That's because it's about the taste.

It is rich, rewarding, complex and very much in the full-bodied, sherried style we've come to associate with The Dalmore. It's smooth, well-mannered and a good demonstration that while age matters, it's not everything in great whisky. Look for plums and chocolate on the nose and spice, coffee and Christmas cake on the palate.

However, you'll probably pay around £125–£150 a bottle. So sip it slowly, probably after dinner, and, while you're at it, put your feet up and check your share portfolio.

[11] Actually, I made that up.

Nose   Citrus notes, like kumquats; ripe plums and dark chocolate.

Taste   Spices, coffee and rich fruit cake come through, presumably influenced by the various wine casks. It's rich, heady stuff.

Finish   Back come the citrus notes, with some lovely wood and vanilla to end with.

Verdict ....

....

66

The Glenlivet
Nàdurra 16 Year Old

Producer	Chivas Brothers Ltd
Distillery	Glenlivet, Ballindalloch, Banffshire, Scotland
Visitor Centre	Yes
Availability	Specialists, duty free, possibly better supermarkets and distillery
Price	◻◻◻

www.glenlivet.com

The Glenlivet
Nàdurra 16 Year Old

Owners Chivas Brothers (part of the giant French group Pernod Ricard) have been making big strides recently with The Glenlivet, which is particularly popular in the USA. The distillery has been expanded and there are a number of different styles available.

Glenlivet is one of the most distinguished names in Scotch whisky history. So highly regarded was it that, for many years, rival distillers took to hyphenating the word Glenlivet on to their own brand name. Eventually, one distillery won the legal right to call itself 'The Glenlivet' and this is it.

It was also famously one of the very first distilleries to take out a licence after some important legislation in 1823 so, completely immodestly, it now styles itself as 'the single malt that started it all'.

But that's not why this is here. There are two reasons to try this: first of all, it's a classic Highland whisky; and second, this particular expression is bottled at cask strength. Regular The Glenlivet is mainstream, but the extra strength and body really appeals to enthusiasts.

That's because the connoisseur wants to get as close as possible to the whisky in the barrel and so looks for a product bottled without any chill filtration (which tends to remove body) and at cask strength. It costs a little more because of extra tax but, if you think about it, it goes a lot further.

The Glenlivet Nàdurra (which means 'natural' in Gaelic) is matured in first-fill, ex-bourbon American oak casks, resulting in a lovely creamy taste. It is released in batches; expect to find it at around 55% abv. Try some – but be sure to sip it carefully at first!

Nose   Fresh wood shavings, with apple and pineapple notes. Floral.

Taste   Soft fruit and honey; some oak wood, pears and menthol hints.

Finish   A markedly dry finish, with ginger, oak and nuts.

Verdict ....

....

67

Producer	
Distillery	
Visitor Centre	
Availability	
Price	

The Glenrothes 1995 Vintage
The Edrington Group
Glenrothes, Rothes, Speyside,
Scotland
Sadly, no
Specialists and some supermarkets
◻◻◻

The Glenrothes
1995 Vintage

The Glenrothes, hidden away behind the less than exciting main street of Rothes, wasn't the first distillery to release vintages, but proprietors Berry Bros & Rudd (Edrington own the distillery, but BB&R the brand) were the first to do so whole-heartedly. And what a success it has been.

Ironically you may find their Select Reserve is easier to get hold of but it is worth persevering. The older vintages, now in the distillery's phrase 'extinct' (they've run out), command a premium in the collector's market, fetching £400 and more. It's nearly £700 for the limited edition John Ramsay Legacy, which commemorates their recently retired Master Blender, one of the nicest men in the whisky industry, but you don't need to pay that.

Take this very tasty 16-year-old 1995 Vintage. It should set you back around £45 and, as the most recent release, it shouldn't be too difficult to get your hands on a bottle. Interestingly, the 1995 Vintage was the first specifically laid in cask with the intention of, when mature, bottling as The Glenrothes. The vintages sold before this were made using existing stocks, otherwise destined for the blending vat.

With about 30% from first-fill American sherry oak delivering butterscotch, some first-fill Spanish sherry oak providing spice and dried fruits, and the rest from refill casks, the characteristic Glenrothes balance and complexity of flavour is achieved. It is a 'come hither' whisky, easy to sip at 43% abv and very consistent with the nose.

All the front labels carry quite clear and detailed tasting notes, enabling you to find the style you particularly favour. Interestingly, the tasting notes on the early vintages were signed by R. H. Fenwick, though later editions carry John Ramsay's signature. Colleagues fondly remember the shaggy-haired Fenwick for his dogged personality, bloodhound nose and fondness for long walks. His 'nose' was reputedly more receptive than that of any of his colleagues, almost super-human in its sensitivity, and it's clear from the casks he selected that he enjoyed a sherry finish.

If you can sniff out a Fenwick bottling you've identified a very rare puppy indeed. Meanwhile, enjoy this 1995.

Nose   Very fresh and floral; slightly herbal; Callard & Bowser toffees.

Taste   An attractive fruit basket to open; developing some spicy smoke hints.

Finish   Dried fruits, fading to lemon curd.

Verdict ....

....

68

Producer
Distillery

Visitor Centre
Availability
Price

The Glenturret 10 Year Old
Highland Distillers
Glenturret, Crieff, Perthshire,
Scotland
Yes
Limited specialists and distillery
☐☐

www.thefamousgrouse.com

The Glenturret

10 Year Old

It would be very easy to write off Glenturret as a giant tourist operation, with a tiny distillery stuck somewhere in the middle. And it's true that the presence of The Famous Grouse's 'brand home' does rather overwhelm this modest little operation, hidden down a picture-book glen just outside Crieff – which itself is something of a magnet for coach tour operators.

There is the Famous Grouse 'brand home': a Disneyesque 'Flight of the Grouse' experience (best experienced before tasting too generously); lots of displays; a Famous Grouse tasting bar; a large shop; another tasting bar; and a restaurant. It's probably also true to say that if The Famous Grouse marketing team hadn't decided to plough money into the tourism side of the operation, the distillery would have been closed or, like Glengoyne, Bunnahabhain and Glenglassaugh, been sold off by Highland as they concentrate on The Macallan and Highland Park.

And yet…and yet… There are things here to capture the attention of the keenest malt aficionado, and I don't mean the rather kitsch statue of Towser the mouser.[12] Yes, there are even some whisky enthusiasts who don't realise this is where you can find the only manually operated mash tun in Scotland. (To be fair, you have to be totally hard-core to know that; Charlie MacLean told me and he should know.)

Seriously, it is a great pleasure to see a distillery operating on this scale. Something about these Lilliputian operations makes the process easily understood by even the neophyte visitor. They may have planned simply to get some whisky marmalade for the woman next door who kept an eye on their cat, but they come away with a better appreciation of everything that goes into whisky from Glenturret's miniaturised scale.

And here's another thing, whisky fans: they're making a peated spirit there these days called Ruadh Maor (not Mhor, I asked). It's all reserved for The Black Grouse at the moment, but who knows….

[12] Exactly why you would wish to draw attention to the remarkable number of vermin running about the place escapes me, but that would seem to be the implication of a statue to commemorate the distillery cat for its Guinness World Records entry as a prodigious mouse catcher.

Nose   Gentle citrus and vanilla. Bourbon influence evident.

Taste   More citrus; dried fruit and peel; honey.

Finish   Gently rolling and sweet.

Verdict ....

....

69

Producer	
Distillery	
Visitor Centre	
Availability	
Price	

Bain's Cape Mountain Whisky
Distell Group
James Sedgwick, Wellington,
Western Cape, South Africa
No – but visitor centre planned
Specialists
▢▢

www.distell.co.za

Bain's
Cape Mountain Whisky

With a strong indigenous wine-making industry and many years of economic isolation, it should be no surprise to learn that South Africa has a substantial and well-established distilling industry. Add to that the fact that since the country rejoined the world community, Scotch whisky sales have been booming there once again (historically, this was an important market for blends such as Dewar's and Johnnie Walker, and today South Africa is Scotch's fifth largest market by volume) and one could predict the rise of local whisky distilling.

The James Sedgwick distillery can be traced back to 1886 and they began making whisky in 1990. Considerable expansion, based on their Three Ships brand, is in hand as their whisky continues to enjoy local success.

What one might not have predicted is that a grain whisky would emerge from South Africa that is both remarkably good and remarkably good value. This is Bain's Cape Mountain and, without putting yourself to very much trouble, you can pick up a bottle in the UK for under £30. If it helps to overcome your reticence, you might like to know that this was awarded a Gold Best in Class from the International Wine & Spirit Competition in 2010, which is a useful mark of quality.

The Cape Mountain grain is double-matured in specially selected oak casks and bottled at 43% abv. After the initial 3 years' maturation period, it is released from the wood and then once again re-vatted into oak casks for a further 2 years' maturation. Curiously, unless you looked very hard at the bottle, you wouldn't know this was a grain whisky. There is some small wording on the capsule and copy on the side of the bottle, but otherwise it is rather coy about its origins, which seems a shame.

Grain whisky can be quite fine, in a subtle and refined way, and makes a refreshing change from some heavier blends or more full-flavoured single malts. While not the most challenging whisky you'll ever try, this is a great example of the style and a credit to its producers.

Nose Apricots, toffee and vanilla. Quite understated.

Taste Soft, sweet and spicy.

Finish Sweet notes linger, then gently fade.

Verdict ....

....

70

Producer
Distillery

Visitor Centre
Availability
Price

Three Ships 10 Year Old
Distell Group
James Sedgwick, Wellington,
Western Cape, South Africa
No – but visitor centre planned
Specialists
■■■

www.threeshipswhisky.co.za

Three Ships

10 Year Old

One of the things about making single malt whisky is that – in general – you have to wait a long time until it's really ready. Even in climates warmer than Scotland (that'll be most of the world, then) maturation can't be hurried and years are needed to achieve the complexity that comes with real maturity. Which is one reason why a lot of vodka is distilled ('Not a drop sold until it's cold,' as they say) and why a number of small craft distillers release their new make: it makes for a source of ready cash.

So it takes a well-founded and substantial operation to wait ten years to release any whisky, let alone a South African single malt. This comes from the Distell group, makers of Bain's Cape Mountain (see number 69). There are many wonderful things about this whisky, not least the fact that it is distilled by a former Derbyshire county cricketer (a left-handed batsman – 16 innings in 12 first-class matches with an average of 27.36, in case you cared; you don't get this sort of information in just any old whisky book).

Andy Watts, for it is he, then played in South Africa but trained with Morrison Bowmore in Scotland and took up the Manager's position at the Sedgwick distillery in 1991. He would appear to know what he's doing.

But back to the whisky. It was first released in 2003 but sold out quickly and was not available again until 2010. The earlier version was finished in sherry casks but here they have opted to use 100% American oak.

This is a limited release but, such has been the reception, as demonstrated by the impressive number of international awards for this whisky, that you can expect more to become available as they build stocks. Judging by the website, the distillery is an impressive operation with a handsome pagoda-topped building at its heart.

And so, to Mr Watts we say, 'Well played, sir!' We look forward to your second innings. You've quite bowled us over.

Nose   Dried fruits, vanilla and some smoky hints.

Taste   Ripe fruits (peach); mouth coating with spices; robust.

Finish   Oak wood and honey; just crosses the boundary ropes for an elegant 4.

Verdict

71

Producer	Distilleries and Distributions Liber
Distillery	Liber, Padul, Granada, Spain
Visitor Centre	Yes
Availability	Limited specialists and distillery
Price	◻◻◻

www.destileriasliber.com

Embrujo de Granada

Liber is not the only whisky distillery in Spain (DYC in Segovia is both substantially larger and longer established) but it was the first to produce single malt. And, like any distillery, it makes much of its water source and the wooden casks it uses for aging. The end product is known as Embrujo de Granada – 'Bewitched by Granada'.

Located in Granada, near the Sierra Nevada Mountains, the distillery was established by a small group of enthusiasts supported by friends and family as investors. The stills were created by local craftsmen but closely resemble Scottish pot stills, with a large boiling ball, but with very tall straight necks and shallow lyne arms.

Great stress is placed on cask selection and extended maturation. Casks are American oak barrels previously used for Xerez wine (sherry). If you work through their website and find the English version, there is a little video which shows very clearly the colour effects of maturation at various ages.

The website further explains that: 'some of the gaps between the slopes of Sierra Nevada and the Costa Tropical have a microclimate [with] alternating temperatures, below freezing winters and hot summers, which gives our own character and personality [to the] whisky.'

It also claims that maturation differs from Scotland in that there is little or no loss of alcohol as the volume decreases; and one might expect a faster maturation period in Spain, due to higher summer temperatures.

Production started in 2002 but there is no age statement on any bottles that I have seen. Between the colour and the taste, one imagines it to be around 5 years of age, or possibly slightly older.

As with many smaller distillers, a range of other liqueurs, rum and vodka is also produced. As an example of the worldwide interest and enthusiasm for single malt whisky, and proof that it can – with care – be produced virtually anywhere, Embrujo de Granada is of more than passing interest to the enthusiast and a welcome entrant on the world whisky scene. I was certainly bewitched by it.

Nose   Light, floral and honeyed. Wine notes.

Taste   Raisins, dark fruits and rich Christmas cake. Chocolate and vanilla essence.

Finish   Nicely balanced.

Verdict

72

Producer
Distillery
Visitor Centre
Availability
Price

Mackmyra Brukswhisky
Mackmyra Svensk Whisky AB
Mackmyra, Valbo, Sweden
Yes
Specialists and distillery
⬜⬜⬜

www.mackmyra.se

Mackmyra

Brukswhisky

Mackmyra has been a sensational success and has inspired, at the time of writing, a further five boutique whisky distilleries in Sweden. Most are small and supplies have yet to find their way out of the domestic market, other than in extremely limited quantities.

But Mackmyra is well on the way to becoming much more than a boutique operation, having started work on the ambitious 'Mackmyra Whisky Village' at Gävle, a few miles from the present distillery. When complete, this will represent a £50 million investment that will quadruple production capacity and provide a radically new distillery, increased storage and a visitor centre. All this is part of a 10-year grand plan which will see exports increase to around 50% of output. The first phase opened in December 2011.

Mackmyra is currently available in the UK, Canada and the USA and, as I write, the company is seeking a foothold in Taiwan and China. All of this is good news because their interesting and very high-quality whisky will become easier to find.

True to their innovative attitudes, Mackmyra tend to release a number of different expressions, but two core styles can be identified, one somewhat reminiscent of Speyside, with a fruity style, and the second clearly inspired by Islay. But do not be deceived by the slight gesture of obeisance to Scotland: this whisky has its own very distinct and unmistakable style; the smoky signature of the latter coming from Swedish juniper wood and bog moss, not the peat of the Hebrides.

However, they now offer an entry-level style called Brukswhisky ('Everyday Whisky'), which is matured for approximately 5 years in first-fill bourbon casks and then vatted with spirit aged in sherry casks and Swedish oak. Then, to pep things up, a little of the smoky Mackmyra is added. This is bottled at a rather unorthodox 41.4% abv and is naturally coloured and non-chill filtered.

But be careful: if you get a bottle of this you're going to want *lots* of their other whiskies and they are not cheap!

Nose   Floral, with spices and cereal. Has been criticised as 'light' – I'd say delicate.

Taste   Oak, pears and pepper dance round here; then a chocolate and honey sweetness kicks in.

Finish   Lingers; some astringency towards the end.

Verdict ....

....

73

Producer
Distillery

Visitor Centre
Availability
Price

Whisky Castle Edition Käser
Käsers Scholes AG
The Whisky Castle, Elfingen,
Switzerland
Yes
Limited specialists and distillery

www.whisky-castle.com

Whisky Castle
Edition Käser

Put away your cynicism. Forget the jokes about chocolate and cuckoo clocks. Don't dare mention *The Third Man*. Believe it or not, there are around a dozen distilleries making whisky in Switzerland. You can be forgiven for not knowing about this, though, since firstly, they're all small and, secondly, whisky couldn't be distilled there legally until July 1999.

However, I was so sceptical that I went to visit one of the very first and best-known distilleries – The Whisky Castle at Elfingen – where they started making whisky immediately the law was changed. Like a number of small distillers, they made their first few batches in the stainless steel still normally used for fruit schnapps (at which, incidentally, the Käser family excel). Being perfectionists, they weren't happy with the result, so they invested in a dedicated copper pot still – believed to be unique in Switzerland.

Nothing had quite prepared me for the pure delight of the distillery itself, though, which has been constructed in the style of a traditional American Shaker barn, and also accommodates a small restaurant for pre-booked groups, a galleried bar and a dramatic picture window through to the warehouse. It is all thoroughly admirable.

Many different whiskies are produced there, some highly experimental. Snow Whisky, for example, was made entirely with water from melted snow off the Jura mountains, and Full Moon is produced with water drawn only on the night of the full moon. It may sound like New Age nonsense but Ruedi Käser had the water analysed and it is clearly different from the normal flow. They also make an intriguing Smoke Rye and a whisky using spelt. Is this whisky? I'm not sure, but it tasted fine.

The flagship expression is the Edition Käser, bottled at approximately 5 years of age and at a hard-hitting 68% abv. Most is, of course, sold in Switzerland, but supplies have been exported to Germany, The Netherlands, Austria and China. I include it here with the earnest hope that you visit and that an enterprising retailer will soon arrange to sell at least one of these whiskies in the UK. Discussions are, I believe, in hand.

Nose   A dramatic spicy and herbal nose, with underlying fruit.

Taste   Huge alcohol delivery but soft and creamy with water; fruit and honey notes.

Finish   Lingering and consistent.

Verdict ....

....

74

Producer
Kavalan Classic
King Car Corporation
Distillery Kavalan, Yuan Shan, Taiwan
Visitor Centre Yes
Availability China, SE Asia and Japan; EU and USA from 2012; and distillery

Price ▢▢▢

www.kavalanwhisky.com

Kavalan Classic

There's a new star in whisky's firmament – and it's not from Scotland or Kentucky. Nor is it from Japan or Ireland, or any of the world's traditional whisky-producing nations.

Surprisingly, Kavalan Single Malt comes from the distinctively named King Car Corporation in Yuan Shan, a city in the north of Taiwan.

The history of the distillery is, by Western standards, staggering. Observing the local passion for whisky, King Car's Chairman T. T. Lee decided to build a distillery – Taiwan's first – as recently as 2005. He flew his technical crew and R&D team to Scotland, hired a consulting team and started work. Fast.

Right from the start, this was an impressive operation, able to make up to 9 million bottles annually. The distillery combines the best of traditional techniques, with pot stills manufactured in Scotland, alongside innovative engineering and automation. Next door is the huge visitor centre, able to host more than 24,000 visitors a week – over 1 million visited last year alone; that's more than all of Scotland's visitor centres combined.

The first whisky was released in 2008 and astonished experts. It's been widely acclaimed. A panel of skilled tasters in a blind test for *The Times* of London placed it above a number of Scotch whiskies of a similar age. It has won international awards and whisky bloggers worldwide have singled it out for special praise.

The reason that such a young whisky can perform so remarkably well is a combination of the distillery's design, great cask selection and the rapid speed of maturation in Taiwan's intense heat and humidity. Storage conditions there contribute to very high rates of evaporation and it's possible to bottle remarkably mature-tasting whisky in just 3 to 4 years. It's only going to get better, and quickly, too.

There is something here to please every whisky connoisseur; it's clear that the Master Distillers of Scotland and Kentucky have a fight on their hands!

Nose   Rich and warming; sweet with citrus hints and ripe fruits (peach and mango).

Taste   Liquorice; sweet and appealing; mouth coating with wood notes; light fruit cake and peaches and cream.

Finish   Smooth, round and consistently appealing. The liquorice note lingers nicely.

Verdict

....

....

75

Producer Beam Inc.
Distillery Jim Beam, Clermont Distillery, Kentucky, USA
Visitor Centre Yes
Availability Specialists and distillery
Price ◻◻◻

Baker's 7

www.smallbatch.com

Baker's 7

Small batch bourbon is, basically, America's answer to single malt Scotch – or, at least, it was until rye's recent revival snatched its cult status. Releasing these small batch styles certainly worked in terms of bringing greater attention to the category and allowing some premium pricing. And, in fairness, some rather interesting and enjoyable products were made that got people talking about bourbon again after years in the doldrums.

It's not exactly a strictly defined category but at its heart is rigorous barrel selection and picking out particularly high-quality spirit which, through some vagary of the warehouse (perhaps nothing more than its exact position in the racks), stands out from the crowd. 'Perfectly formed' might be a better definition, were it not for the unfortunate connotations of that phrase (if you don't know, don't ask).

Back in the late 1980s, the originators of the style were Beam Inc., not exactly a boutique distiller, and with Knob Creek, Basil Hayden's, Booker's and Baker's 7 they aimed to capture something of a pre-Prohibition character to the whiskey. Having drunk a very small quantity of whiskey from that era, I can see what they're getting at. Fortunately, you can get a bottle of any one of these for the price of a dram of the really old stuff (assuming, that is, you can find any).

In trying to explain the character of Baker's, the distillery themselves say that it is aged 7 years and bottled at 107 proof; it utilises a special strain of jug yeast that has been in the Beam family for over 60 years and which results in a silky smooth texture and consistent taste from batch to batch. *Whisky Magazine* rated it the World's Best American Whiskey in 2007, though some commentators would maintain that at 7 years old it is getting a little long in the tooth.

The Clermont distillery is home to the T. Jeremiah Beam House and the Jim Beam American Outpost. Guess what: you can buy stuff there like a Jim Beam folding chair; a coffee mug; a pool cue; or even a branding iron with custom letters. Be still my beating heart!

Nose   Lots going on – plenty of ripe fruit and chocolate, for example.

Taste   Complex and deep, with loads of spice and a *pain au chocolat* note.

Finish   On and on it goes, with a smashing chocoholic crescendo.

Verdict

....

....

76

Producer
Distillery

Visitor Centre
Availability
Price

Blanton's Original Single Barrel
The Sazerac Company
Buffalo Trace, Franklin County,
Kentucky, USA
Yes
Specialists and distillery
□□□

Blanton's
Original Single Barrel

In a moment of singular incompetence I missed this out of the first *101 Whiskies* book. It's nice to be able to make amends.

This, after all, is the original single barrel bourbon and that marks a hugely significant moment in whiskey history. This launch, in 1984, represents the point at which someone realised that bourbon could – just possibly – be turned around in popular esteem. Bourbon's history and single malt whiskies provided the business model for doing it.

We should also credit Colonel Albert Bacon Blanton (a 'Kentucky Colonel', not a military fellow – but what a moniker!) who for 55 years kept the Buffalo Trace distillery running through Prohibition, flood and war. Apparently he bottled the choicest barrels from Warehouse H for private distribution to friends and privileged visitors. Though he died in 1959, the tradition lives on and the Single Barrel releases are, to this day, taken from this near–sacred hot spot. His acolyte Elmer T. Lee, now Distiller Emeritus at Buffalo Trace, was responsible for the initial selections and is still closely involved despite his advanced years.

You can love or hate the bottle with its ornate stopper featuring a horse and jockey. Apparently there are eight to collect, with an initial letter spelling out Blanton's and each dramatising a different moment in a horse race. Well, it does come from Kentucky.

More importantly, Blanton's is revered by bourbon drinkers and has collected a hatful of awards. No wonder. Though every release is, by definition, different, they have been greeted with universal acclaim – and with some gratitude by the rest of the industry who have happily imitated the single barrel concept and the premium pricing that goes with it.

That's probably the only downside to these products. But then, you won't be drinking them every day and your friends will appreciate you for pulling out a bottle on special occasions.

No specific tasting note because the bottle you find will almost certainly be different from the one in front of me as I write, but look for a sweet, full-bodied taste profile, with hints of nuts, caramel, orange and light chocolate.

If you really want to splash out and can track some down, there is also a Gold Edition and a cask strength version.

Verdict

77

Producer
Distillery
Visitor Centre
Availability
Price

Buck Bourbon
Frank-Lin Distillers Products Ltd
Their lips are sealed
No
Limited specialists

www.frank-lin.com

Buck Bourbon

'Keep your bourbon smooth and your spurs sharp,' say the owners of Buck, a little-known (well, it was to me) Kentucky straight bourbon. But then, try as I might, I couldn't find out very much more on the web or in any of the standard books on American whiskey.

It was the label that first appealed and piqued my curiosity; charmingly poised on that delicate balance between 'authentic' and 'kitsch'. It features a black-and-white photograph of a cowboy riding a bucking bronco under the legend 'ranch hand certified'. Perhaps the very ranch hand on the label was endorsing it, though he looks as if he's got his hands full. If he tries to drink it like that he's going to spill the lot, I thought. It brought back childhood memories of Roy Rogers and *The Lone Ranger*, so I just had to try some.

And I will admit to being pleasantly surprised, especially as it comes at a tasty 45% abv. After that, it all got a bit mysterious. Frank-Lin Distillers Products (not, I think, distillers themselves) are based in California, but Buck is unequivocally described as 'Kentucky Straight Bourbon Whiskey', which means it's made for them in that state. As we will see from some other brands listed here, there's nothing particularly unusual or sinister in that, it's just slightly surprising that they keep it such a closely guarded secret.

Nothing to worry about, though. It's not as well-known as the big brands but it's a perfectly sound buy if your taste runs to a slightly sweeter than normal tipple, with faux-nostalgic packaging (the bottle is slightly suggestive of Four Roses and has an attractive 'period' look).

Fact is, it may be a stranger in town, with hints of a young Clint Eastwood, but it's a darn fine whiskey for all of that. Try and lasso some for the next time you find yourself out on the lonesome trail rounding up steers.

Nose   Ripe vine fruits and peaches. Cereal and menthol.

Taste   Full-on sweetness (but add some ice); vanilla and toffee to the fore, then mint. Mixed spice and oak.

Finish   Smooth, round and warming, with some nice spice notes, but just a slight tannic note as it fades.

Verdict ....

....

78

**Buffalo Trace,
White Dog – Mash #1**
(also Wheated Mash and Rye Mash)

Producer	The Sazerac Company
Distillery	Buffalo Trace, Franklin County, Kentucky, USA
Visitor Centre	Yes
Availability	Limited specialists and distillery
Price	◻◻◻

www.buffalotrace.com

Buffalo Trace

White Dog – Mash #1
(also Wheated Mash and Rye Mash)

This White Dog, as the Americans refer to their new make spirit, is the bourbon equivalent of the Georgia Moon Corn Whiskey (see number 85).

The Buffalo Trace distillery is one of the best-known and most highly regarded in Kentucky, with a loyal following of enthusiasts. At the risk of over-simplifying, the White Dog product is the alter ego of the finished whiskey.

The three styles are designed to illustrate the distillery's three main mash styles: Mash #1 for their bourbons, such as Buffalo Trace and Eagle Rare; Wheated Mash, used to make W. L. Weller and Pappy Van Winkle; and Rye Mash, used to make Sazerac. It's been something of a fashion to release new make, often at fancy prices (be aware that this is no exception): Bruichladdich, Highland Park, Kilchoman and Glenglassaugh, among others, have done this. For a small, newly opened distillery (which these guys are not) it's a great way to excite interest and, more importantly, bring in some badly needed cash. But presumably Buffalo Trace just saw an opportunity to join in the fun after watching a number of small-scale craft distilleries in the USA release an equivalent product.

Apart from the curiosity value, though, what do you actually use this stuff for? Well, enterprising cocktail experts have been mixing it into some innovative and truly unusual cocktails where the very high strength has some value and, er, that's about it.

Rather than buy a whole bottle yourself (even allowing for the fact that it comes in a half-bottle size), you might want to consider buying this with friends and using it to kick off a tasting session. Nothing will more clearly demonstrate the role of barrel aging and the impact of good wood on whiskey. After which you can quickly move on to the proper stuff!

That might include Buffalo Trace's remarkable series of releases known as the Single Oak Project which, sadly, there is hardly space to mention, let alone discuss. Sorry.

Nose   Huge alcohol delivery at first; then cereals and some light spice notes.

Taste   Sweet and spicy; syrupy; more complex and developed than the Georgia Moon.

Finish   Takes your breath away!

Verdict

79

Producer
Distillery

Visitor Centre
Availability
Price

Bulleit Frontier Whiskey
Bulleit Distilling Co.
Four Roses, Lawrenceburg,
Kentucky, USA
Yes
Supermarkets
▢

www.bulleitbourbon.com

Bulleit

Frontier Whiskey

Well, apparently there really was an Augustus Bulleit in Louisville, Kentucky, who created a small batch bourbon for his bar 'sometime in the 1830s'. Then unfortunately he went missing in 1860 while transporting casks from Kentucky to New Orleans (why he was taking whiskey to New Orleans when his bar was in Louisville isn't explained).

And there the story might have ended, except that his great-great-grandson Tom stepped in. A lawyer by profession, Tom's lifelong dream had been to revive the family's bourbon legacy. And he actually did that in 1987, so let that be an example to you. Today, of course, the brand is owned by Diageo, but Tom still pops up from time to time as a 'Brand Ambassador'. And, just to confuse matters a little further, it's actually distilled at Four Roses which, of course, is owned by Kirin, one of their competitors.

You don't have to swallow any of that to enjoy this easy-drinking, rye-laden whiskey, though it does add to the pleasure just a little bit. And you don't want to pick a fight with Tom because he served in Vietnam with the US Marine Corps.

The taste is somewhat off the mainstream because the recipe calls for rather more rye than usual, which has led to the development of a Bulleit Rye, produced by Lawrenceburg Distillers and only recently available in the UK (worth a try). Actually, the original recipe was around two-thirds rye, which would mean that today it couldn't be sold as bourbon anyway. It's been reduced to under 30%, which is still high, and which accounts for the peppery note.

Though there is no age statement, the whiskey is said to be 6 to 8 years old, again quite a respectable vintage. At 40% abv it works well as a cocktail base, where it really sings for its supper. But I'd like to see the strength restored to the original 45% abv.

By the by, the used barrels end up in Scotland where they're put to good use maturing single malts for Diageo's blends.

Nose   Fresh and lively, fruity and sweet. Great wood notes and orange zest.

Taste   Vanilla and honey, with citrus undertones.

Finish   Hints of spent fireworks, drinking chocolate and that vanilla again.

Verdict ....

....

80

Producer
Distillery

Visitor Centre

Availability
Price

Evan Williams 23 Years Old
Heaven Hill Distilleries, Inc.
Bernheim, Louisville, Kentucky,
USA
Yes – company Heritage Center
in Bardstown, Kentucky
Specialists and distillery
☐☐☐☐

www.evanwilliams.com

Evan Williams

23 Years Old

Just to prove that they can do packaging (compare this to their efforts on Rittenhouse and Pikesville Rye), Heaven Hill have managed a rather more attractive presentation for their Evan Williams range. It's not showy, especially flamboyant or dressed up in boxes[13] and fancy cartons, but it does look as if someone cares, even on the standard expression (which is a good value, easy-drinking bourbon that many rate very highly for its price).

Then you can get various premium offerings, including the 1783 No 10 Brand, a single barrel vintage or you can try their Kentucky Liqueur in cherry or honey flavours. They also make an egg nog (I didn't try it – sounds horrid to be honest).

All of this is built on another of those slightly contrived heritage stories that all distillers' marketing people seem to love, in this case a wonderfully romantic tale of a Welshman, Evan Williams, described as 'entrepreneur, politician and distiller', who lays claim to being Kentucky's first distiller.

But – even giving Evan the benefit of the doubt – I question if he would have ever produced anything quite as remarkable as this 23-year-old masterpiece, unquestionably the flagship of the range.

This is an extraordinary age for bourbon and, even more wonderfully, it has held on to lots of strength, still coming in at 107 proof (53.5% abv). Master Distillers Parker and Craig Beam pick up a treasured family legacy here, including the celebrated jug yeast strain perfected by the legendary Earl Beam. Williams may have been Kentucky's first distiller but they are surely among its finest.

So, even though it's one of the more expensive bourbons recommended here, you get a lot for your money and I'm confident that you won't be disappointed. In the words of the song, there's definitely a welcome in the hillside but it's not Wales' rolling pastures, it's the blue grass of Kentucky. Evan would be very happy, indeed, to see this carry his name.

[13] If you really want a box, they do a limited edition, distillery-only bottling that you can get at the Heritage Center.

Nose   Intense dark fruits and espresso, with dark chocolate shavings.

Taste   So much body here, with oak and all the promised delivery from the nose arriving in a rush.

Finish   Rolls on and on.

Verdict ....

....

81

Four Roses Yellow Label

Producer	Four Roses Distillery LLC
Distillery	Four Roses, Lawrenceburg, Kentucky, USA
Visitor Centre	Yes
Availability	Specialists, some supermarkets and distillery
Price	☐

Four Roses

Yellow Label

Distiller Rufus Rose may have been the first to market a Four Roses, but it was Paul Jones Jr who trademarked the name in 1890, claiming production and sales back to the 1860s. He had moved his grocery business to Louisville, Kentucky, where he opened on Main Street's historic 'Whiskey Row' in 1884. Various romantic stories are attached to the naming of the brand but, of course, it was all changed by Prohibition anyway.

Today Four Roses is an American icon, though surprisingly is owned by the Kirin Brewery Company of Japan. But, credit where it's due, they have proved themselves benevolent owners, investing in the brand and opening up new markets. Most important of all, they reintroduced Four Roses to its homeland, where the previous owners had withdrawn it from sale.

There are a number of expressions available, including a Single Barrel, which is probably the pick of the bunch, and a tasty Small Batch collection. By definition, both of these will change over time but they have generally attracted very positive comment. Neither is particularly expensive so it's hardly a great gamble to pick one up if you do see it.

What you will find easier to get, and which is really very well priced, is the 'entry level' Yellow. This is aged for 5 years and represents a great starter bourbon. In 2011, for the second consecutive year and for the third time in 5 years, Four Roses Distillery was named 'Whisky Distiller of the Year – America' by *Whisky Magazine*'s international judging panel, who also praised the private barrel selection programme.

Don't be deceived by the modest packaging (why American distillers can't run to nicer closures defeats me) and the low price: this punches above its weight and will stand up well against some better-known brands. Of course, modest packaging and low price might be two sides of a coin. Just a thought, if there are any marketing people reading this…

Folk who really know bourbon praise this highly.

Nose Honey, burnt toffee and some fruit. Cereal notes.

Taste Smooth and creamy; spice and oak notes, with apple and pear hints.

Finish A slight astringency cuts the sweetness and adds a welcome tart note at the end.

Verdict ....

....

82

Producer
Distillery

Visitor Centre
Availability
Price

Gentleman Jack
Brown-Forman Corporation
Jack Daniel's, Lynchburg,
Tennessee, USA
Yes
Widespread
⬜⬜

www.jackdaniels.com

Gentleman Jack

I couldn't bear to include standard Jack Daniel's here. Too boring, too ubiquitous and too heavily curated a marketing story. You don't hear a lot about Nearest Green (Google him because I don't have room) and, like a certain extremely popular white rum, the brand is everything. I'm far from certain that the majority of drinkers even know what it is they're drinking. Or care, for that matter.

Not 'bourbon' for sure, though you'll hear it called that. This is Tennessee whiskey and eventually I concluded that it deserved a mention. After all, they sell lots of it and this is the kind of fashionable product that introduces new drinkers to whiskey. If you can look past the Disneyfied 'good ole boy' patter, there is a certain charm to the visitor centre and museum at Lynchburg.

Gentleman Jack is a sort of upmarket Jack, the principal difference being that it runs through the charcoal filter twice (20 feet in all). So it's a little smoother. But that's it really.

It's pretty easy-drinking stuff; not too demanding and, given the distillery's scale, I would suggest it can hardly be as 'rare' as the label suggests. For all the homespun charm from the tour guides (which I find feels heavily scripted), this is a very large distillery indeed, so they're unlikely to run out any time soon.

But I don't suppose anyone would be offended if you asked for this, though no one's going to be particularly impressed either. I saw a consumer's tasting note on one well-known whisky retailer's website which read: *'I'm not a whisky drinker but I had a taste of this as a tribute after a funeral. Extremely smooth with no after taste. Impressive!'*

So, actually, I'm wrong. Non-whisky drinkers are impressed. Serving suggestion: keep a bottle on hand for the non-whisky drinkers in your life and for funerals. We can't have them drinking vodka and it saves the single malt for you.

The mention of funerals reminded me of the late, great Michael Jackson whose early death was a sorry loss to the world of whisky. As a modest tribute, these are his tasting notes from *Whisky Magazine* (thanks to them).

Nose   Soft but insistent. Sweet then dry. Burnt brown sugar and charcoal. Slightly less overt charcoal-phenol than the regular Jack Daniel's.

Taste   Smooth. Very toasty. Dryish start, but becoming surprisingly sweet. Spicy. Syrupy background.

Finish   Cinnamon. Lemons. A slightly richer and more restrained interpretation of Jack Daniel's.

Verdict

83

Producer
Distillery

Visitor Centre
Availability
Price

George Dickel Barrel Select
George A. Dickel & Co
Dickel, Tullahoma, Tennessee,
USA
Yes
Specialists and distillery
◻◻◻

www.dickel.com

George Dickel
Barrel Select

Well, as they say, 'If you only know Jack, you don't know Dickel' and I suppose it's true that there are a good few folk out there who are blithely unaware of Tennessee's other distillery. But then, they probably think Jack Daniel's is a bourbon. *You* wouldn't make that mistake (not now anyway).

Just to confuse matters a little further, Dickel label their bottles as containing 'whisky' in the Scottish manner. That's allegedly because founder George Dickel thought the water at Cascade Hollow made their whisky the equal of any Scotch, but since he never actually visited the Hollow and never made a drop of either whiskey or whisky in his life, that story owes more to marketing than actual history. But what was it with these Tennessee pioneers – Mr Jack famously died from blood poisoning brought on by a broken toe after he'd kicked the office safe (like kicking the bucket, only better paid), and George D. fell off his horse, though it took him six years to hand in his feed bag.

And the morral[14] of that story? Your guess is as good as mine; so on to the whiskey, sorry whisky.

This is the flagship expression, originally created to mark the distillery's reopening in 2003. If you want to know more about the company's rather chequered and colourful history, skip over the official website and find a series of articles on Chuck Cowdery's blog (he's an expert on American whiskey – and American whisky as well). It's made slightly differently from that other Tennessee whiskey but the details are too laborious to get into here – it's all to do with charcoal.

Diageo own Dickel these days but seem more interested in promoting Bulleit Bourbon, which is a shame. But it means that you can show off your whisky knowledge by picking up a bottle of this underrated and little-known sipping whisky. It's not easy to find in Europe but a few specialists carry it and it's worth the money.

[14] You knew, of course, that a 'morral' was a type of nose bag for a horse. You didn't? Do try and keep up.

Nose   Cooked cereals, honey and bananas.

Taste   Notably smooth, said to be due to the filtration process; more fruits, vanilla and mint.

Finish   Well-mannered with lingering sweet spices.

Verdict ....
....

84

Producer
Distillery

Visitor Centre
Availability
Price

George T. Stagg
Straight Bourbon
The Sazerac Company
Buffalo Trace, Frankfort, Kentucky, USA
Yes
Limited specialists
▢▢▢▢

www.buffalotrace.com

George T. Stagg
Straight Bourbon

Standard bearer of the Buffalo Trace Antique Collection this is a HUGE whiskey. A monstrous, roller-coaster, blockbuster of a flavour, George T. Stagg is an annual release that was first launched in 2002. Such is its reputation that there's generally something of a stampede for the latest bottling – it's usually in the shops by September each year (though in 2005 they surprised everyone with an additional spring release as well).

Be aware that outside its home territory it's not cheap. Expect to pay over £100 a bottle in the UK. Even for a cask strength whisky of 71.3% abv in the slightly larger US bottle that's hardly a bargain, though the current (2011) release is over 18 years old – and that's a lot for a bourbon.

As enthusiasts will know, the Buffalo Trace distillery is one of Kentucky's finest and the George T. Stagg releases have accumulated a staggering number of awards in their short life. It would be tedious to list them all; suffice it to say that any number of well-informed critics rave about this product. Most recently it was named Best Bourbon and collected a Double Gold Medal at the San Francisco World Spirits Competition 2011.

But go carefully: it is a very full-bodied whiskey. The producers suggest that you 'add a few drops of mineral water, sit back and ponder the wonders of the universe.' Well, that's never a bad plan where great whisky is concerned, though I'd suggest trying it neat first, and then adding water steadily, perhaps ending up with more than a few drops (it can take it).

You'll be rewarded with rolling waves of flavour. Critics talk of coffee, honey, oak, cinnamon, cloves, redcurrant jelly, dark orange marmalade, liquorice… the list is almost endless. Whatever you want to find is here, it would seem, except any trace of over-age, woodiness or flabbiness.

A genuine American classic. Tasting notes are for the 2011 release; you may well find the 2012 in stores now.

Nose Maraschino cherries, vanilla, spice and Christmas cake.

Taste Intense espresso, 70% dark chocolate, oak, butterscotch/caramel, corn, honey, red fruits and citrus notes – they just keep coming.

Finish After a while your head is spinning, not with the alcohol, but simply the bewildering array of aromas and tastes.

Verdict ....

....

85

Producer	**Georgia Moon Corn Whiskey** Johnson Distilling Company (Heaven Hill Distilleries Inc.)
Distillery	Bernheim, Louisville, Kentucky, USA
Visitor Centre	Yes – company Heritage Center in Bardstown, Kentucky
Availability	Limited specialists
Price	

Georgia Moon

Corn Whiskey

You've got to try this! Moonshine, guaranteed less than 30 days old, and it comes in a preserves jar, like the one your granny used to pickle onions. You'd swear it came straight from some hillbillies right out of *The Dukes of Hazzard*, except this isn't going to poison you and there's no need to keep an eye out for the cops. Though you could always soak off the label before serving it to your friends at a Prohibition-themed party. That should sort the men from the boys.

As the company explains, corn whiskey of this style is: 'the forerunner and kissing cousin to bourbon… defined by the US Government as having a recipe or mash bill with a minimum of 81% corn, the rest being malted barley and rye. Today, Heaven Hill is the sole remaining national producer of this uniquely American Whiskey style.' Actually, I think Philadelphia Distilling make something called XXX Shine from corn, but we'll let that pass.

So, if you want to understand how whisk(e)y starts out life, what the 'good ole boys' (and probably your great-grandfather) drank, exactly what cask maturation adds to new make spirit, or you just want to try a great American tradition – this is the stuff for you. Honest, unpretentious and cheap and cheerful, it's by no means as horrible as you expect it to be! After a couple, you'll wonder what everyone was so worried about.

Perhaps sadly, it's been watered down somewhat to a rather tame 40% abv. For the full experience you should be drinking this straight off the still in the open air before heading off to a NASCAR meet. But in our sanitised, health-and-safety age this is as close as you can legally get to bootleg spirit.

However, judging by the number of home-made stills you can buy on a well-known internet auction site, the tradition would appear to be flourishing in them thar hills, but this saves you a lot of trouble. Definitely don't try this at home!

Because the knowledge that you won't go to jail and won't go blind is a great comfort .

Nose Popcorn and cooked cereal.

Taste Initially sweet and rounded, then some spice notes develop. Cocoa. Slightly oily (that's good).

Finish It's off and away before you can say, 'Howdy doody, sheriff.'

Verdict ....

....

86

Producer
Distillery

Visitor Centre

Availability
Price

High West Rendezvous Rye
High West Distillery
High West like to keep this a secret
but I have my suspicions that it is
Lawrenceburg, Indiana, USA
Yes – brand home is in Park City,
Utah
Limited specialists and brand home
□□

www.highwestdistillery.com

High West

Rendezvous Rye

Here's a whiskey that's not been without its share of controversy. Though bottled under the High West label, this wasn't actually distilled there. All we're told is that the stocks were 'sourced' with assistance from Jim Rutledge of Four Roses, though they didn't necessarily emanate from there either. That very mild secrecy – if secrecy it was, because I think the answer can be discerned from digging through the website – aroused the ire of some hard-core aficionados, despite the acknowledged quality of the product, wherever it came from. My suspicions are that it is Lawrenceburg Distillers, Indiana, but that would be telling!

Whatever, it has won a hatful of awards: *Malt Advocate* (now *Whisky Advocate*) scored it very highly and made it one of their Top Ten Whiskies of 2008; it picked up a Double Gold at the San Francisco Spirits Competition in the same year; and in 2010 the American Distilling Institute rated it Best Rye Whiskey. So what is it?

Apart from the fact that we're not supposed to know where it was made, technically this is a blend of two very different ryes: a straight 6-year-old with a mash bill containing 95% rye and 5% barley malt; and a straight 16-year-old with a mash bill containing 80% rye, 10% corn and 10% barley malt. Just to add to the fun, it is non-chill filtered and bottled at 92 proof (46% abv).

With such a dramatically high rye content you get a very traditional style and a full-on flavour delivery that initially takes your breath away. It's little surprise that it's been so well received in competitions.

Proprietor David Perkins established High West in 2007, to become Utah's first licensed distillery for nearly 140 years. After setting this very high benchmark with Rendezvous and some 'sourced' whiskey, a growing legion of fans have high expectations of him and his team.

If their sensitivity to the architectural restoration of the historic buildings of their home is anything to go by, the distillery is in good, thoughtful hands.

Nose   A big, spicy nose with loads of burnt sugars.

Taste   Huge initial impact and mouth feel; loaded with spice and mixing freshness and vitality with the depth and dignity of age. Almonds and mint notes.

Finish   Sustained and complex.

Verdict

87

Hudson Manhattan Rye

Producer	Tuthilltown Spirits
Distillery	Tuthilltown, Gardiner, New York State, USA
Visitor Centre	Yes
Availability	Limited specialists and distillery
Price	▢▢▢▢

www.tuthilltown.com

Hudson

Manhattan Rye

This is beyond weird. In Tuthilltown at night they play loud rap music on a continuous loop to help the barrels age. It's not New Age mumbo-jumbo but the shrewd observation that the low frequency bass notes cause the spirit to vibrate, thus promoting uptake of colour and flavour from the wood. It's just one of the innovative things coming out of this New York State craft distillery.

For around 220 years Tuthilltown Gristmill milled local grain into flour. In 2001 Ralph Erenzo and Vicki Morgan acquired the property and with the help of partner Brian Lee, they converted one of the mill granaries to a micro-distillery. Two and a half years later, Tuthilltown Spirits produced their first batches of apple vodka and by 2006 they were making whiskey, including two bourbons, a single malt and this rye. It very soon garnered an exceptional reputation.

In June 2010 William Grant & Sons acquired the Tuthilltown Hudson whiskey brands (though not the distillery itself) and took over their international distribution, presenting the opportunity for a worldwide breakthrough.

Historically, New York State was known for rye whiskey, the basis of a classic Manhattan. But Prohibition put a stop to that, until these guys came along and surprised everyone. As production expands, any batch-to-batch variation will be evened out but, unless something very strange and untoward happens, you should be sure of a superb product.

As the poster child of the craft distilling movement, Tuthilltown has won a number of awards and this flagship Hudson Rye has also collected a number of medals and commendations.

Be aware that it's bottled in a 37.5cl bottle (that's just over half a standard UK bottle) at 46% abv. The equivalent bottle cost is around £90 so you won't be drinking this every night. But, if you save it for a treat, then the night you do open it will automatically become special.

Crackerjack stuff from a relatively new US craft distiller that's about to get some serious exposure. Breaking with convention because I loved this, I'm including some tasting notes – these are for Batch 5 from 2011.

Nose   Bittersweet grains and liquorice. Vanilla and citrus hints.

Taste   Richly spiced and immediately engaging; toasted wood; curry spice then fennel and aniseed. Quite dry. Charred wood.

Finish   Some smoke in the finish, with minty notes in the background.

Verdict

88

Producer

Distillery
Visitor Centre
Availability
Price

Jefferson's Very Small Batch
McLain & Kyne Ltd
(Castle Brands Inc.)
They won't say!
No
Limited specialists
⬜⬜

www.mclainandkyne.com

Jefferson's

Very Small Batch

To be completely honest, this is a bit of a mystery. I picked it up at my local off-licence (The Drinkmonger, Pitlochry – very good, by the way) because I vaguely remembered that it had won some sort of a medal or something. To my very great surprise, the staff at The Drinkmonger didn't know much about it either (which is very unusual), but they assured me that it was good. The medal turned out to be a San Francisco World Spirits Competition Gold in 2008 and various respected US commentators had nice things to say about this small batch bourbon as well.

So I looked it up online and found the usual fairly bland marketing stuff about the distilling traditions of the ancestors of the McLain & Kyne company which, lo and behold, I then found repeated more or less verbatim everywhere else I looked. That suggests that every other writer was as baffled as I was but didn't trouble themselves to find out any more. But read on…

After going round in circles for a while, I established that McLain & Kyne aren't actually distillers. The company was established in 1998 by Chet Zoeller (well-known author on bourbon) and his son Trey, and they started out by finding small parcels of stock which they bottled under the McLain & Kyne label. McLain refers to Martha McLain, who was reputedly an energetic bootlegger (with six children to support, as well, she was kept busy); still no idea where Kyne fits in. In late 2006 they sold the company to Castle Brands Inc., where Trey still works nosing out barrels of stock for Jefferson's.

As he describes it: 'I buy esoteric lots that are too small or too niche for other distillers.' Well, I like small and niche. It's what makes the whisky business interesting and fun.

Today there are three Jefferson's bourbon expressions, including Presidential Select, which is a very rare 17-year-old from the legendary Stitzel-Weller distillery, and a recently launched rye. But what you'll find most easily, at least in Europe, is the Very Small Batch, their 'entry level' offering.

And very good it is, too.

Nose   Sweet pecans and vanilla. Peaches and cream.

Taste   Nuts, great, smooth, mouth filling caramel and fruit mix.

Finish   Lingers agreeably, but some will find it cloying.

Verdict

89

Producer
Distillery
Visitor Centre
Availability

Price

Jim Beam Black
Beam Inc.
Clermont, Kentucky, USA
Yes
Specialists, supermarkets
and distillery
☐

www.jimbeam.com

Jim Beam

Black

Beam Inc. was relatively recently floated on the New York Stock Exchange (October 2011) as a specialist drinks company, where previously it had been part of a larger conglomerate. No sooner was that listing complete than industry pundits began forecasting that Beam would be swallowed up again by one of the industry giants – Diageo or Pernod Ricard were the favourites. That would be a sore end for a company that can trace its ancestry to 1795.

So far, at the time of writing, that hasn't happened and Beam have surprised the industry by buying Cooley of Ireland and launching some interesting and innovative products, such as Red Stag (see number 90). Hopefully they can continue as an independent operation and carry on adding interest and variety to the whiskey market.

Standard White Label Jim Beam, though the best-selling bourbon in the world (don't write in – Jack Daniel's is Tennessee whiskey), is the basis for this Jim Beam Black. But Black is a great deal more interesting and well worth the relatively modest premium charged for the additional 4 years of aging in charred oak casks matured in Kentucky's barrel houses.

Except that we Europeans don't get the 8-year-old stuff; by and large they keep that for the domestic market. Instead, 'our' Jim Beam Black is 'triple aged' – a rather coy way of saying it's 6 years old, that being three times the minimum age for bourbon. You might find it misleading and assume that 'triple aged' referred to three types of wood. An understandable mistake, but legally that can't be done with bourbon.

Having said all that, a few specialist whisky retailers have tracked down supplies of the older version and that is really the one you want – so check your label carefully and accept no substitutes. It's been a regular award winner at San Francisco and, for a crowd-pleasing, easy-to-drink bourbon with a little more to offer than the run of the mill brands, this works very well.

Nose   A classic – White Label but with more attitude.

Taste   Buttery smooth, some tobacco smoke hints and lots of wood and spice. Liquorice and vanilla.

Finish   Not the most extended ever; pleasantly suggestive of a cigar you once smoked.

Verdict

90

Producer
Distillery
Visitor Centre
Availability

Price

Jim Beam Red Stag

Beam Inc.
Clermont, Kentucky, USA
Yes
Specialists, supermarkets
and distillery
☐

www.jimbeam.com

Jim Beam
Red Stag

Why would you take a perfectly decent 4-year-old bourbon and infuse it with black cherry flavour? Because you were feeling bored? Because you could?

Of course not. Beam's corporate website makes it perfectly clear why they've done this. It's to provide 'a fresh, contemporary taste that appeals to both long-time Jim Beam fans and new consumers who may not have previously considered the bourbon category.' The last bit is the important bit: in reality, hard-core bourbon drinkers and whiskey purists will throw up their hands in horror. But they won't stop drinking the regular stuff, so there's very little risk in trying something a little far out. Or so the US and Canadian whiskey industry thinks: because of legislation, as I explain elsewhere (see number 91), you can't do this with Scotch.

But flavoured vodkas and rums have been eating whiskey's lunch for some time now in established markets and the new consumers in the emerging BRIC regions have no set prejudices to guide them. So they'll try most things. These flavoured alcohols are easier to drink, mix well and their generally sweeter taste appeals to a less-experienced palate. Let's face it, whisky/whiskey is something of an acquired taste and not everyone wants to put in the necessary work when there are many more immediately appealing alternatives out there.

So Jim Beam Red Stag (and Jack Daniel's Tennessee Honey, Revel Stoke and others) are products designed to provide an easy and accessible route into more mainstream whiskies. It may or may not work, but then believe it's worth trying. Personally, the idea fills me with dismay but then there's no reason why my tastes should dictate what other people drink.

And if it does encourage people who 'don't like whisky' (you do meet them occasionally) to try a little drop rather than vodka or rum, then why not? It's almost as cheap anyway. You could keep a bottle on hand to try and convert the unbelieving to the cause of real drinking. It's noble work.

Nose   Marzipan and, yes, black cherry.

Taste   Pretty cloying frankly, far too sweet for me – but then, I'm not the target audience.

Finish   I did manage to finish it, though.

Verdict

91

Producer
Distillery

Visitor Centre
Availability
Price

Maker's Mark Maker's 46
Beam Inc.
Maker's Mark, Loretto, Kentucky,
USA
Yes
Specialists and distillery
□□□

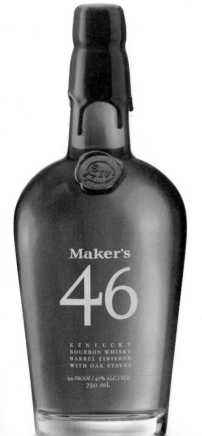

Maker's Mark
Maker's 46

Now this is the type of thing that would get you drummed out of the regiment in Scotland, and yet, at least for me, it typifies a restless spirit of innovation and experimentation that has been lost as a result of the pedantic application of regulations built on a distorted view of 'traditional practice'. Note: not everyone agrees with this point of view.

First of all, understand that Maker's Mark is something of a cult brand. Not quite as under the radar as once it was, but still, it's a drinker's drink.

What happens with Maker's 46 is that the distillery takes barrels of fully matured Maker's Mark, ready for bottling, empties them and puts the whiskey to one side. Then they pull the top off the barrel and fix ten new, specially treated staves of French oak inside it. They don't serve any structural purpose, but are simply there to add flavour. Then the whiskey is put back into its original barrel, with the added staves, and left to mature for several more months. Then it is bottled at 47% abv, a little stronger than 'regular' Maker's (admit it, you were expecting 46% abv – well, so was I).

The effect of the toasted staves is to add extra toasted oak and caramel flavours, and the result of bottling at a higher strength is to beef up the mouth feel. It's the first 'new' Maker's in 50 years and has proved hugely popular. Good for them.

But if you tried this with Scotch whisky the sky would fall in. Ask John Glaser of Compass Box who essentially did this with the first batch of his Spice Tree. Drinkers loved it but, under pressure from the Scotch Whisky Association (SWA), it was withdrawn.

Wine makers do this, Kentucky bourbon distillers do this, but Scotland can't. According to the Compass Box website the SWA's view is that: 'Quality is completely irrelevant.' They had their interpretation of the law, which held that what Compass Box was doing was not 'traditional', so that was the end of the story.

Not for Maker's 46, though.

Nose   Burnt toast, caramel and vanilla.

Taste   All the ginger, caramel and oiliness of the standard product but enhanced and more complex. Liquorice, loads of cereal and more weight.

Finish   Perhaps on the sweet side for the European palate but satisfying nonetheless.

Verdict

92

Producer
Distillery
Visitor Centre
Availability
Price

Old Crow Reserve
Beam Inc.
Clermont, Kentucky, USA
Yes
Specialists and distillery

www.beamglobal.com – but silent on poor old Old Crow

Old Crow
Reserve

Old this, old that… they're mighty fond of the senior citizenry in Kentucky, but this ole fella is the oldest of the old. And for a good while it looked as if it had been pensioned off to the great still house in the sky. This, indeed, seems to be the fate of many classic whisky brands – their owners appear to lose interest and watch with detached curiosity as a once-renowned name slips into genteel poverty.

Perhaps, if it's fortunate, it will acquire cult status or simply retain a vestige of popularity, clinging on as 'No. 2 Blend in Uruguay' or some such far distant market. Then the owners' nice PR lady will greet you with an embarrassed smile when you enquire after its health.

Old Crow seemed to be going that way. The name honours a Scot called Dr James Crow, who arrived in Kentucky in 1823 apparently to escape a somewhat disreputable past. Whatever misdemeanours he had committed, he turned out to be a skilled distiller and for the next few decades worked round the industry perfecting bourbon's sour mash method.

Presidents and Generals enjoyed his whiskey, though he never actually owned a distillery himself – the Old Crow plant at Glenns Creek (now abandoned) was built after he died. The brand's decline seems to date from a recipe change in the 1960s and, following its sale to Jim Beam in 1987 and the closure of the distillery, one might have been forgiven for concluding that Old Crow was, in fact, a dead parrot.

However, in 2010, on the back of bourbon's general revival, an improved version, Reserve, was launched. This is aged for an additional year (4 as opposed to 3 for the standard style) and, at 86 proof (43% abv), it is a little stronger. Let's be honest, it is still a 'value' offering, but it is a step in the right direction and, though it's next to impossible to track down in most of Europe, I include it here as a modest salutation to its eminent history and as a gesture of encouragement to the proprietors.

What's more, back in the day, there was an Old Crow Rye. Now that would be something to crow about (sorry).

Nose   Oak and vanilla. Popcorn.

Taste   Rather sweet – try some ice and a mixer.

Finish   Some burn, unless you've added that ice.

Verdict ....

....

93

Producer
Distillery
Visitor Centre

Availability
Price

Old Fitzgerald 1849
Heaven Hill Distilleries, Inc.
Bernheim, Louisville, Kentucky, USA
Yes – company Heritage Center in
Bardstown, Kentucky
Specialists and distillery
◻◻

www.heavenhill.com

Old Fitzgerald 1849

Like a number of American whiskies mentioned here (and, indeed, like a lot of American whiskies not mentioned here), Old Fitzgerald seems to do its best to undersell itself with drab packaging. It's a mystery. From the nation that invented marketing, it really isn't good enough. If only they took a few lessons from the Scotch, Irish or even the Japanese distilling industry, they could probably get a few more dollars per bottle.

Oops! Let's keep that to ourselves, for the price here belies the value in this distinctive bourbon, famously made with the 'whisper of wheat' introduced by then-owner Pappy Van Winkle (American distilling aristocracy, in case you didn't know). By substituting wheat for rye, the result is a softer, less spicy whiskey which is distinctively smooth.

Since Van Winkle owned the brand, there have been many changes of ownership and even a switch in distillery, after a spectacular fire in 1996 destroyed the distillery at Bardstown (the Heritage Center and a giant warehousing complex remains there). They seem to have managed a remarkable consistency in flavour, though, which is no mean achievement.

That the Old Fitzgerald line carries on is another example of the benefits of the continuity that comes from family ownership. In this case, the hands of the renowned Shapira family and their father and son distilling team, Parker (still going strong after 50 years in the business) and Craig Beam. They tend to favour older whiskeys and this Old Fitzgerald variant has an average of 8 years in wood before bottling. If you like it, there is also a 12-year-old expression to be found.

Not a whiskey to change your life (if such a thing exists) but a solid, reliable bourbon with a wheated twist to add interest.

Nose   Burnt maple sugars, honey and vanilla.

Taste   Liquorice, honey and dark chocolate. Loads of vanilla and caramel notes; a hint of smoke and some spice.

Finish   Hardly profound or complex but lasting.

Verdict ....

....

94

Producer
Distillery
Visitor Centre
Availability
Price

Old Forester
Brown-Forman Distillers Company
Shively, Louisville, Kentucky, USA
No
Specialists
🟦🟦

www.oldforester.com

Old Forester

Is it possible that in today's world of brand management and cost control a whiskey could be saved by sentiment? It hardly seems likely but this may just be the exception that proves the rule.

Old Forester was first created in 1870 by George Garvin Brown, founder of the Brown-Forman dynasty and, from the first, it bore his signature on every bottle. Which was unusual because, at that time, very few whiskies came in bottles. Brown, having worked in pharmaceutical sales, understood the importance of the sealed container and the reassurance that this offered to the consumer. And thus a great firm was born.

But, over the years and particularly after Prohibition, sales of Old Forester declined and brands such as Jack Daniel's and Early Times took over. However, in a family-controlled company, it's hard to kill off something as closely associated with the beginnings of the firm and, despite the fact that Old Forester acquired something of a blue collar image and was sold at what we'll politely describe as 'value' prices, it was allowed to stagger on.

And then, a few years ago, people started to cotton on to what great value this was. The product's quality had never been compromised and, as bourbon started a slow renaissance, Old Forester was once again appreciated; especially as its close links to Woodford Reserve began to be more widely understood.

So the company started to pay more attention to this old favourite and now, as well as the Classic 86 Proof (43% abv), we can enjoy Old Forester Signature and a Birthday Bourbon (an annual limited release). They are all still great value, especially the Classic.

Perversely, the more expensive styles are more widely available in Europe, but none are exactly over-priced for the quality and stylish presentation. Perhaps it's one to collect on your next vacation to the land of the free. You can be sure it will find an appreciative audience when you get it back to Blighty, especially when you recall this brief history and impress all concerned with your arcane knowledge of whiskey lore.

Nose   Complex spices and vanilla; burnt sugar and oak.

Taste   With a higher-than-average rye component, loads of spice, then fruit and vanilla.

Finish   All the nose and taste stays with you.

Verdict

95

Producer
Distillery
Visitor Centre

Availability
Price

Pikesville Straight Rye Whiskey
Heaven Hill Distilleries, Inc.
Bernheim, Louisville, Kentucky, USA
Yes – company Heritage Center in
Bardstown, Kentucky
Specialists and distillery
▢

www.heavenhill.com

Pikesville
Straight Rye Whiskey

Crikey! Even by the convoluted standards of American whiskey history this is a tangled mess. I'm not even going to try to explain this in detail so, if you're interested, look it up. But pour yourself a large measure first and be prepared for your brain to hurt even before you start drinking.

Here's the short version: once upon a time Pikesville was made in Maryland, but now it's not. In fact, it comes from Heaven Hill's giant Bernheim complex in Kentucky, where Rittenhouse Rye, among others, is also made.

It's supposed to replicate a pre-Prohibition Maryland style, though it's anyone's guess what that really tasted like. Like Rittenhouse, the presentation gives the impression that the company really don't care all that much: the boring, standard, tall, circular bottle is hardly enhanced by the rather dull label, and certainly not at all set off by the nasty plastic closure.

Still, look on the bright side – although they don't make a lot of it, it's cheap as chips, really full of spice and bite, and is great in cocktails. So keep it out of sight from your friends and pretend that it's something a great deal rarer and more expensive when you serve it up. They'll believe you.

In the right mood I could drink rather too much of this, either neat (it's a humble 80 proof, 40% abv and surprisingly smooth, despite the spices) or in a cocktail, particularly if you like them on the dry side.

That's all folks. Just buy some.

Nose   Crisp, sharp, clean; cereal notes and ginger.

Taste   Fresh, relatively delicate but with agreeable spice notes.

Finish   Fades a little quickly but, hey, did you see the price?

Verdict ....
....

96

Producer Luxco
Distillery Bernheim, Louisville, Kentucky, USA

Visitor Centre No
Availability Limited specialists
Price

Rebel Yell

www.rebelyellwhiskey.com

Rebel Yell

A no-nonsense, unpretentious Kentucky straight bourbon, Rebel Yell represents pretty fair value at a typical UK price of around £30. While hardly the most complex or demanding of bourbons, sometimes you just want a drink to sip, savour and not have to puzzle over. Having said that, it was a Double Gold Medal Winner at the 2011 San Francisco World Spirits Competition. So someone clearly loved it.

Depending on which story you believe, the brand was originally created by W. L. Weller around 1849 – or was it actually first named 100 years later? The truth is that, as with so many bourbons, it underwent various changes of ownership and the origins no longer really seem to matter. Today it is distilled under licence as a wheated bourbon for the (relatively anonymous) Luxco Corporation by Heaven Hill at their Bernheim distillery.

Originally it was released as a 6-year-old product and sold exclusively in America's Deep South, where presumably the Confederate imagery still had some resonance: the 'rebel yell' was a war cry used by Confederate soldiers to instil fear, presumably in their enemies, while engaged in battle. That's not very nice, is it? You could get thrown out of most bars for that.

Anyway, it proved sufficiently popular that by 1984 the new owners decided to take it national, and then international, subtly changing the marketing from 'exclusively' to 'especially for the Deep South'. Today, it's a non-aged product and, with the passage of time, the fearsome battle cry just seems like a rather romantic memory. There's still quite a scary-looking cavalryman in full charge on the label, though.

Apparently Keith Richards of The Rolling Stones ('popular musical performers, m'lud') was partial to the odd drop. He introduced it to Billy Idol ('a "punk rock" musician, apparently, m'lud') which subsequently gave him the title of his best-selling LP. I can't really see that this is particularly important but I drag it in for fans of the rock music school of whisky journalism.

In fact, it's totally redundant, if you ask me, but it seems to amuse some people. As we know, there's no accounting for taste.

Nose   Honey, vanilla and dried fruits.

Taste   Full bodied and rich; very consistent with first impressions of the aroma. Easy-drinking and silky.

Finish   Smooth, round and warming, with some nice spice notes.

Verdict ....

....

97

Producer
Distillery
Visitor Centre

Availability
Price

Rittenhouse Rye 100% Proof
Heaven Hill Distilleries, Inc.
Bernheim, Louisville, Kentucky, USA
Yes – company Heritage Center in
Bardstown, Kentucky
Specialists and distillery
□□

www.heavenhill.com

Rittenhouse Rye

100% Proof

Here's a whiskey that goes out of its way to disguise its quality. First, consider the nasty plastic cap, then ponder the crudity of the label (I wonder – can anyone at brand HQ actually have *looked* at this in the last 50 years?); marvel at the absence in this wired world of a dedicated website; and finally contemplate the mystery of the price. At under £30 it isn't actually cheap (though it does its best to look it) but it's hardly premium either.

What is this bottle telling us? 'Look away,' it seems to say. 'Nothing interesting here. You're better off with one of those trendy designer bottles over there.'

And that's a shame because, although distilled now in Kentucky, it carries a famous old name from the great days of rye distilling in Philadelphia.

Finding out exactly who distils it today takes a little bit of detective work. On the back label you'll find the enticing description, 'Distilled by D.S.P. KY354' or possibly KY-1. Decoded, that's US terminology for Distilled Spirits Plant (oh, the romance of it) Number 354 in Kentucky. Such a title suggests a failing North Korean tractor collective but actually refers to the Early Times distillery in Louisville, home of Old Forester Bourbon. However, previous supplies came from Bardstown and, with demand for rye whiskey suddenly increasing, distillation recently switched to Heaven Hill's Bernheim Distillery (hence, KY-1). So, if you find a bottling you particularly like, you might want to stash a few bottles just in case the taste changes too much.

This is excellent stuff – great neat and fabulous in cocktails. '100' refers to proof strength, thus 50% abv, giving the whiskey real body and mouth feel (makes it better value, too), and that's perfect in a rye Manhattan.

Not for nothing was it awarded World's Best American Whiskey at *Whisky Magazine*'s World Whisky Awards 2010 – but you have to appreciate that this competition is judged 'blind', meaning the panel don't see the bottle.

Which, in this case, was probably just as well.

Nose   Some pepper bite, then cloves and cinnamon buns.

Taste   Sweet burnt sugar, then layers of evolving, teasing, intriguing spices.

Finish   More spice, some last pepper prickle. Satisfyingly complex.

Verdict ....
....

98

Producer
Distillery
Visitor Centre

Availability
Price

Templeton Rye
Templeton Rye Spirits, LLC
Lawrenceburg Distillers, Indiana, USA
Yes – brand home is in Templeton,
Carroll County, Iowa
Limited specialists and brand home
▢▢▢▢

Templeton Rye

'To a regular guy, from the boys.'

So read the inscription on Al Capone's personal cocktail shaker. Curiously, when last seen it was resident in a Devon country house, alongside Lord Nelson's teapot.

The Templeton Rye folks would have you believe that this is the kind of thing Al Capone drank when he wasn't bootlegging into speakeasies. And, to that end, the website features some rather charming YouTube-style home-made videos featuring members of the Kerkhoff family whose relatives distilled it back in the day and a veritable small army of the senior citizens of Iowa labelling bottles. They seem to be having quite a big day out. Perhaps Iowa is like that.

Officially, it's only available in Iowa, Illinois, San Francisco and New York, but I tracked down a bottle in London so you can get it. Now, without wanting to spoil the fun (and I'm a sucker for a good story) the product may have started out life on an Iowa farm but today it's actually made by Lawrenceburg Distillers in Indiana and, in my opinion, has travelled rather further from Al and the boys than the cocktail shaker has from Chicago. Having been launched as recently as 2006, it would appear to have precious little to do with the 1920s product, though in fairness there is apparently a recipe somewhere on a faded scrap of paper and they do plan to bring distilling back to Iowa.

Actually, I can't imagine that it really needs all this faux-heritage stage dressing because this is a cracking drop of 90% rye grain whiskey that can – and should – stand firmly on its own merits. It's strange, because the website provides an extraordinary level of detail on sales but is absurdly coy on where it's made.

Perhaps the fact that it has already won notable awards and critical praise should encourage them. In my view, whiskey enthusiasts deserve the facts. If you're not careful, you end up believing the marketing.

I've been there and it can get messy.

Nose   Spice, leather and toffee.

Taste   Toffee and sweeter spice notes. Delightfully full.

Finish   Nice balance.

Verdict ....

....

99

Producer	
Distillery	**W. L. Weller 12 Year Old**
	The Sazerac Company
	Buffalo Trace, Frankfort, Kentucky, USA
Visitor Centre	Yes
Availability	Specialists and distillery
Price	□□

www.greatbourbon.com

W. L. Weller

12 Year Old

This grand old brand can trace a lineage back to William Larue Weller, a Kentucky distilling pioneer, and later to the renowned Stitzel-Weller distillery where it was made for many years. This was purchased by Diageo, who closed it in 1992 following construction of their Bernheim distillery, which they subsequently sold. Today, lacking representation in American whiskeys and, as far as I can see, having little immediately obvious interest in their own Dickel brand, Diageo prefer to promote Bulleit, which is made for them by Four Roses. Go figure.

Anyway, W. L. Weller is now owned by The Sazerac Company and produced at their Buffalo Trace Distillery, a fair contender for a contemporary Stitzel-Weller if ever there could be such a thing. Dave Broom describes it as 'a university of straight whiskey distillation' and Buffalo Trace is noted for its meticulous barrel selection, driven mainly by the location of individual casks on different floors of their maturation warehouses.

Ever since 1849, the Weller style is for a wheated bourbon. There aren't too many examples of wheated bourbon so this 12-year-old version could make it into this selection on that alone. But, in fact, it's here on its own merits as a rather fine, subtle and complex whiskey that offers great value, especially considering its age.

I'd keep this for drinking on its own, rather than mixing or using it in a cocktail. There's simply too much quality – too much going on in the glass to compromise or dilute it, other than perhaps with a little water (it's a healthy 45% abv). Raise a glass to a whiskey legend and the gentle softening effect of a little wheat.

If you ever visit Kentucky, be sure to take the tour at Buffalo Trace. They have a range of alternatives to suit your interest, budget and timetable, and it is one of the highpoints of any bourbon tour.

Nose   Somewhat oily but appetising; some cereal notes. Honey and almonds.

Taste   Initially dry, then soft and fairly sweet but never cloying. Opens up with time to offer plums, caramel/fudge and crème brûlée.

Finish   More cereal, oak and honey.

Verdict ....

100

Penderyn Madeira Finished

Producer The Welsh Whisky Company
Distillery Penderyn, Brecon Beacons National Park, Wales

Visitor Centre Yes
Availability Specialists, some supermarkets and distillery

Price ☐☐

www.welsh-whisky.co.uk

Penderyn

Madeira Finished

This is the house style of Penderyn, the only whisky distillery in Wales. Apart from its location, the still is rather unusual at Penderyn. They only have one, of their own unique design, which produces spirit at around 92% abv, as opposed to the 60%-odd which would be normal in Scotland.

This, they say, removes certain impurities that traditional pot stills leave behind. That's true. But it's also true to say that these impurities contribute flavour. Now Penderyn doesn't lack flavour, so how do they do it?

The main contributor is their wood regime. The spirit starts off in ex-bourbon barrels (normal enough) and, in this case, is then finished in old Madeira casks. In total, it spends around 5 years in cask, the final year of which is in the Madeira wood. It is then reduced to 46% abv for bottling.

There are lots of different releases in the market (including peated and sherry-wood styles). My recommendation would be to try to find the most recent bottling that you can. That suggests buying through a supermarket where the stock will rotate faster but, if you're really curious, specialists may carry a range of older stock for you to compare. Alternatively, you could try the distillery visitor centre and get the very latest bottlings.

Truthfully, I wasn't terribly excited with the first Penderyns that I tasted shortly after the initial release of stock in 2004. I think they were released too early. But this bottle has made me think again, and I believe that the distillery has now started to hit its stride and release more consistent whisky of a generally high standard. At around £35, it's good value for a niche producer.

It's a really encouraging trend. Penderyn may have started life as something of a novelty but it suggests that there's gold to be found in them there valleys.

Nose   Ripe apricots, then a curious aroma of toasted cheese.

Taste   Quite sweet, with the wood influence apparent. The fruit notes are reminiscent of boiled sweets, with vanilla rounding out matters nicely.

Finish   Astringent and slightly drying, with apricot hints lingering to the end.

Verdict ....

101

Producer
Distillery
Visitor Centre
Availability

Price

Orbis Aged World Whiskey
St James Distillery
A citizen of the world
No
Airport duty free shops, especially
Far East, and some EU ferry lines
▢▢▢

www.stjamesdistillery.com

Orbis

Aged World Whiskey

Let's conclude with something really unusual, confusing and a little bit controversial. This is Orbis Aged World Whiskey – a blend of Scottish, Irish, American, Canadian and Japanese whiskies. The St James Distillery is a marketing company based in London; they don't actually distil anything but simply buy parcels of whisky and blend them together.

Why? You may well ask. Quite possibly, because they can.

According to St James, the inspiration behind Orbis is the concept of 'no boundaries' and they add: *'In developing Orbis, the brand has not been limited by geography, history or convention; our Master Blender has travelled the world in search of the finest whiskeys – in some cases aged 15 or 16 years, although Orbis is not about an aged statement. The result is a product which is unique for the travelling consumer who has a global outlook, is confident, cosmopolitan, broad minded and – like Orbis – not restricted by boundaries.*

'Our main target consumer is the male international business traveller who likes to indulge, is stylish and savvy and enjoys the benefits of globalization in their cosmopolitan lifestyle.'

Sounds like a sort of business version of Alan Partridge.

But once through the marketing gobbledegook, we find a perfectly pleasant and drinkable product. Somehow you feel it ought to be awful, and it certainly offends most of whisky's conventions and protocols but, tasted blind, it's an accessible and appealing whisky that will probably mix well and not offend anyone. Until you tell your purist friends what it is, of course, and then the red mist may well descend.

Just tell them they're not sufficiently confident, cosmopolitan and broad-minded to appreciate it! That should get them talking. And, after all, isn't that what whisky (and this book) is about? I don't necessarily expect you to like Orbis (indeed, you're free to like or dislike any or all of the whiskies here as your taste dictates), but it's worth talking about, especially over a dram.

Nose Smooth and rounded, with a honey sweetness.

Taste Rich and warming; dried fruits and Christmas cake. Some sherry influence, presumably.

Finish It lingers nicely and some smoky hints develop towards the end.

Verdict

102

SPECIAL BONUS WHISKY!

Johnnie Walker Diamond Jubilee

Producer	Diageo
Distillery	What do you care? You're not getting any
Visitor Centre	Yes – brand home is Cardhu Distillery, Speyside, Scotland
Availability	It isn't
Price	If you have to ask…

www.johnniewalker.com

Johnnie Walker

Diamond Jubilee

And now – as they used to say – for something completely different.

This breaks all my rules. There are only sixty bottles for sale, but you can't buy one in a shop. And it costs *at least* £100,000 a bottle. But you can't complain, because you've already had 101 whiskies so this one doesn't count. It's my treat, if you will.

On 6 February 1952, among much pomp and ceremony, a remarkable young woman started the first day of a new job. Queen Elizabeth II acceded to the throne of the United Kingdom of Great Britain and Northern Ireland, and in addition became head of the Commonwealth. Now, long after any normal retirement age, she continues in those demanding roles.

Whatever you think of the idea of monarchy or of individual members of the Royal Family, it can scarcely be denied that this is a remarkable record of public service that few will ever match. A number of distillers will honour it with special editions. None will match Johnnie Walker's Diamond Jubilee.

At virtually 60 years of age it's the oldest Johnnie Walker ever released. Naturally, it was bottled on 6 February 2012, 60 years to the day since her accession, and is presented in a dramatic crystal decanter with a sterling silver collar set with a single diamond. Each decanter is accompanied by a pair of hand-engraved crystal glasses and a personalised leather-bound artifact book, all housed in a bespoke cabinet made of wood from the Balmoral and Sandringham estates.

The Queen was presented with the first of the editions produced. Then sixty further bottles were made available for private sale (that means that if Diageo considered you suitable they offered you the chance to buy one; if they haven't called yet, you can forget it). The price? £100,000. Apparently twenty had gone by March 2012.

Now, if this had just been one of those hyped 'investment' bottles I would never have mentioned it. But Diageo gave all the profit away, guaranteeing at least £1 million to the Queen Elizabeth Scholarship Trust which helps 'enable traditional craftsmanship to flourish in Britain'.

And they sent me a wee taste and let me hold the bottle.

Verdict It was very nice. Trust me. Would I lie to you?

How to taste whisky

Tasting whisky – any whisky – is straightforward. Follow these simple rules to get the most from your dram.

1. Use the right glass. A tumbler is hopeless. What you need is the Glencairn Crystal whisky glass (buy online from www.glencairn.co.uk). If you can't find one, get a sherry copita or brandy snifter to concentrate volatile aromas and help you 'nose' the whisky. The new NEAT™ glass looks, well, pretty neat. More at www.theneatglass.com

2. Fix the aroma and taste with associations – the smell of new-mown grass, for example, a vanilla-flavoured toffee, or the rich taste of fruit cake.

3. Add a little water. It opens up the spirit and prevents your taste buds from becoming numbed by alcohol.

4. Roll the whisky right round your mouth and 'chew' it. Give the flavours time to develop: the whisky has been aging for years – give it as least as many seconds and the rewards will be huge.

5. Finally, think about the 'finish', or the lingering taste that remains. How consistent is it? What new flavours emerge?

Relax, keep practising and you'll very soon discover whisky's unique richness.

How to Use this Book

Imagine you were about to make a trip to a foreign land. Use this book as a sort of traveller's guide to the new country: it points you to some sights that you didn't know were there or might otherwise have ignored on your journey. I don't claim to have all the answers; I don't know what whisky you like and there's no reason at all to assume that you'll like the same whiskies as me. For that simple reason, and because I think the notion of 'the world's best whisky' is both simplistic and reductionist, there are no scores here. For the most part, scores are simply one person's opinion, reflecting their taste and inevitable bias: make your own mind up!

But you can be assured that every whisky here is here for a reason and that they are interesting, challenging, often good and sometimes great whiskies of their kind.

So try them at least once. Before you die.

Further resources

Books

There are many, many books and websites about whisky; some would say too many. However, I have suggested just a few here for further reading, the idea being (like the list of whiskies) to point you in various directions in the pursuit of knowledge.

The first modern book written about whisky was Aeneas MacDonald's *Whisky*, reissued in facsimile in 2006. Despite its age (it first appeared in 1930), it is well worth reading as a poetic general introduction to Scotch whisky that is still surprisingly relevant. His heartfelt plea for transparency in the description of blends and, above all, his championing of single malts when they were all but unknown, mark out MacDonald (*pseud* George Malcolm Thomson) as a true pioneer.

For the history of the Scotch whisky industry, Michael Moss and John Hume's *The Making of Scotch Whisky* is valuable, though dry and now somewhat dated. *Scotch Whisky – A Liquid History* by Charles MacLean is rather easier going. Any title by Charlie is worth reading.

Gavin D. Smith is very strong on the people and personalities in Scotch. Look out for *The Whisky Men*. If you like visiting distilleries, his *Discovering Scotland's Distilleries* has all the information you'll need (but check times by phone if you're travelling a long way).

For taste evaluation of Scotch whiskies try *Whisky Classified* by David Wishart, recently revised and updated.

There is very little in English on Japanese whisky. Perhaps the most authoritative is *Japanese Whisky: Facts, Figures and Taste* by Ulf Buxrud. It does what it says in the title. If there is a really good book on American whiskies it has passed me by and an up-to-date account of Irish whiskey is badly needed.

For more comprehensive coverage of all world whiskies and a basic introduction, look for *World Whisky* edited by Charles MacLean. I was one of a number of contributors. The new edition of the late Michael Jackson's *Malt Whisky Companion* has been compiled by Dominic Roskrow and Gavin D. Smith and is exhaustive. Some people find Jim Murray's annual *Whisky Bible* useful. He tastes almost everything! Finally, *The World Atlas of Whisky* by Dave Broom (a Glaswegian who gets paid to drink) combines comprehensive coverage with authoritative commentary.

The *Malt Whisky Yearbook* is issued annually and covers more than just single malt. It is an invaluable guide: accurate, regularly updated and a mine of interesting information, especially on new distilleries.

All of the above are fairly serious. Though hard to find, *Whisky by Numbers* by Ap Dijksterhuis is the funniest book I know about whisky.

There are various magazines. Perhaps the best (in English) are *Whisky Magazine* (UK) and its American counterpart *The Whisky Advocate* (formerly *Malt Advocate*). *WhiskyEtc* (in Dutch) is first rate. If you read Dutch, obviously.

Websites

There are literally hundreds, perhaps thousands, of websites on whisky, ranging from the exhaustive to the scanty, the authoritative and reliable to the frankly eccentric. Bloggers come and go and maintain their sites with different levels of enthusiasm and accuracy. Virtually every brand of note maintains its own site: if you read between the PR lines there may be some useful information. I've listed the 'official' site for all the whiskies in the book on the relevant page.

Given that the web evolves and changes both rapidly and constantly, the following recommendations may be of limited value. However, for what it is worth, I do look at these sites fairly regularly. Apologies to those that I have missed or forgotten about. A few hours 'Googling' will turn up more whisky sites than you thought possible. Good luck!

www.caskstrength.net In next to no time this has become the blog to watch.

www.forwhiskeylovers.com OK, hands up, I help out with this one.

www.irelandwhiskeytrail.com Guess what this does?

www.maltmadness.com Set aside a good chunk of time if you venture here.

www.maltmaniacs.org I can't imagine how they find the time to keep this up-to-date.

www.nonjatta.blogspot.com Well-informed reports in English from Japan.

www.ralfy.com This is great fun, though whisky pedants can be sniffy about it.

www.whiskycast.com The authoritative whisky podcast – pacy, irreverent, yet respectful.

www.whiskyfun.com 'It's about single malts, music, enjoying life in general.' And so it is.

www.whisky-pages.com Gavin D. Smith's tasting notes and reviews.

www.whiskyadvocate.com A very lively blog here and lots more beside.

www.whiskyintelligence.com News updates and press releases in one handy place.

Where to buy

United Kingdom

In the UK we are spoilt for choice with excellent specialist whisky retailers. The following have particularly good online shopping facilities:

Loch Fyne Whiskies, Inveraray   *www.lochfynewhiskies.co.uk*
Master of Malt, Tunbridge Wells   *www.masterofmalt.com*
Royal Mile Whiskies, Edinburgh   *www.royalmilewhiskies.com*
The Whisky Exchange, London   *www.thewhiskyexchange.com*

But ideally you should browse and talk to some enthusiastic and well-informed staff. There are many more good shops, notably: Arkwrights (Highworth, Wiltshire); Cadenheads (Edinburgh); Lincoln Whisky Shop; Luvians (Cupar and St Andrews); Nickolls & Perks (Stourbridge); Parkers of Banff; Robert Grahams (Glasgow); The Wee Dram (Bakewell, Derbyshire); The Whisky Castle (Tomintoul); Whiskies of Scotland (Huntly); The Whisky Shop (UK wide); and The Whisky Shop (Dufftown – no relation to national chain of same name).

Above all, Gordon & MacPhail's shop in Elgin is a shrine and well worth a visit. In London you will find The Whisky Exchange, Royal Mile Whiskies, Berry Bros & Rudd, Milroy's of Soho and The Vintage House.

France

La Maison du Whisky, Paris   *www.whisky.fr*
(they also have premises in Singapore)
The Whisky Lodge, Lyons   *don't appear to have one*

Germany

There are a good number of excellent whisky retailers in Germany, including:

Cadenheads, Berlin & Cologne   *www.cadenhead.de*
Dudelsack (multiple locations)   *www.dudelsack.com*
Whisky Depot, Hamburg   *www.whiskydepot.com*
Whisky Raritaeten, Wallrabenstein   *www.whiskyraritaeten-langer.de*

Ireland
Mitchell & Son, Dublin   www.mitchellandson.com

The Netherlands
Cadenheads, Amsterdam   www.cadenhead.nl
Van Wees Whisky World, Amersfoot   www.whiskyworld.nl
Whiskyslijterij De Koning, Hertogenbosch   www.whiskykoning.nl

New Zealand
Whisky Galore, Christchurch   www.whiskygalore.co.nz

Russia
Veld 21, Moscow   www.veld21.ru

Taiwan
Kavalan Whisky Showroom   www.kavalanwhisky.com
DRINKS Wine & Spirit store   www.drinks.com.tw

USA
It's a very big country – here are just a few:

Binny's Beverage Depot, Chicago   www.binnys.com
Central Liquors, Washington DC   www.centralliquors.com
Federal Wines & Spirits, Boston   www.federalwine.com
Park Avenue Liquor, New York   www.parkaveliquor.com
The Whisky Shop, San Francisco   www.whiskyshopusa.com
You can also try the list at   www.awa.dk/whisky/wshops/usa.htm

Acknowledgements

My wife, Lindsay, has been enormously patient and, for the second year in a row, put up with my grumpy moods and mental absences while writing this book, so the biggest thanks go to her.

My agent, Judy Moir, believed in the book from the start and was positive, helpful and encouraging. Thanks to her and Bob McDevitt for their enthusiasm and support. Emma Tait and Jo Roberts-Miller did a great job editing the book in double-quick time. The cover was designed by Chris Hannah and Lynn Murdie designed all the pages.

The following (in strictly alphabetical order and profuse apologies to anyone I've inadvertently omitted) helped with samples or background information: James Brown, Rob Bruce, Ian Chang, Ashok Chokalingam, Jason Craig, Ben Ellefsen, Tim Forbes, Donna Hibbert, Ruedi Käser, Larry Kass, Brian Kinsman, Bill Lark, Lars Lindberger, Jim Long, Jari Mämmi, Marcin Miller, Michael Fraser Milne, Dr Nicholas Morgan, Janet Murphy, Stuart Nickerson, Hans Offringa, Bill Owens, Nicol van Rijbroek, Pat Roberts, Katherine Roepke, Ingvar Ronde, Rubyna Sheikh, Sukhinder Singh, Gavin D. Smith, Stuart Smith, Verity Staniforth, Doug Stone, Keir Sword, Jack and John Teeling, Joanie Tseng, Bernard Walsh and Chet Zoeller.

I also bought some whiskies from Royal Mile Whiskies and The Whisky Exchange, both of whom have friendly, helpful and knowledgeable staff.

My grateful thanks to all of them.